CREATING
THE NOT
SO
BIG
HOUSE

Insights and Ideas for the New American Home

CREATING THE NOT SO BIG HOUSE

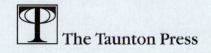

Sarah Susanka

The Taunton Press

PHOTOGRAPHS BY GREY CRAWFORD

With gratitude to all my teachers

PUBLISHER: Jim Childs
ACQUISITIONS EDITOR: Steve Culpepper
EDITORS: Mary Russell, Peter Chapman
COPY EDITOR: Suzanne Noel
COVER DESIGNER: Steve Hughes
INTERIOR DESIGNER: Carol Singer
LAYOUT ARTISTS: Carol Singer, Susan Fazekas
ILLUSTRATOR: Scott Bricher

The Taunton Press
Inspiration for hands-on living®

Printed in the United States of America
10 9

Creating the Not So Big House was originally published in hardcover in 2000 by The Taunton Press, Inc.

The Taunton Press, Inc., 63 South Main Street, PO Box 5506, Newtown, CT 06470-5506
e-mail: tp@taunton.com

Distributed by Publishers Group West

Library of Congress Cataloging-in-Publication Data
Susanka, Sarah.
  Creating the not so big house : insights and ideas for the new American home / Sarah
  Susanka ; photographs by Grey Crawford.
    p. cm.
  Includes index.
  ISBN 1-56158-377-4 (hardcover)
  ISBN 1-56158-605-6 (paperback)
    1. Architecture, Domestic—United States. 2. Architecture, Modern—20th century—United States.
3. Space (Architecture). 4. Interior architecture—United States. I. Title.

NA7208 .S88 2000
728'.0973—dc21   00-044323

Acknowledgments

THE MORE I WRITE, the more I realize how indebted I am to those who have been my teachers—both the people who have taught me in person and those who have taught me through their publications, presentations, and performances. We can only come into our own full flowering by learning from these others who inspire us to express what we Know (with a capital K) with their own knowledge, insights, and way of being in the world. From my kindergarten teacher, to a favorite high school English instructor, to my first architectural design professor, to my many teachers in the art of becoming fully present to all that life offers—all these people have performed such extraordinary service through their efforts. I find myself awed by and deeply grateful for the gifts they have bestowed.

I also want to thank photographer Grey Crawford for his eye for light and space, and for the delight he takes in his work. We developed a rare synergy of intent almost as soon as we began working on the book. Though we'd never met before, we both knew from the first photo shoot that we understood each other's medium and were expressing a similar vision—paring away the superfluous in order to see the beauty beneath. A more perfect fit would have been hard to find.

I am also filled with appreciation for all the people who have worked to bring this book into existence. Before I wrote my first book, I had always assumed that writing was a very solitary pastime, but the reality is quite different. Just as with the performance of a piece of music, it requires not only the composer but an entire orchestra to bring the sound to the ears of the audience. I cannot name everyone here but want to thank a few of this team in particular. Editors Mary Russell and Peter Chapman reviewed, molded, and tailored the text at every turn to make it truly sing. Art director Paula Schlosser and designer Carol Singer gave the book its finely crafted appearance. And acquisitions editor Steve Culpepper and publisher Jim Childs quietly steered from behind the scenes, helping to hone the message to fit its audience. These people are the orchestra, without whom there could be no book. Their diligence, and attention to both the overall vision and the smallest of details, made the whole process into a natural evolution, from the seed of the idea to the pages before you now.

And finally, I want to thank the architects and the owners of the houses illustrated in this book. A home designed by an architect is typically a one-of-a-kind gem, appreciated only by the family who lives there and the friends who visit. The plans are used once and then put in a drawer. Many of the people who hire architects want a "signed original" and enjoy the fact that their home is unique. But for others, uniqueness is not the key. They want a wonderful house that fits them, but if the ideas can be used to benefit others, they're more than happy to have them made available to a larger market. By generously allowing their investments of time, energy, and money to be shared with a broader audience, they make possible this development of a spatial language and the exploration into what makes a house a home. Again, my deepest gratitude.

Contents

Inside the Not So Big House

Introduction

WHEN *THE NOT SO BIG HOUSE: A Blueprint for the Way We Really Live* was published in 1998, I don't think anyone anticipated the avalanche of interest it would generate. Homeowners are clearly more than ready for an alternative to the huge, impersonal "starter castles" that are filling our new suburbs and developments.

Many people wrote me to say that, until reading *The Not So Big House*, they had given up on building a new home because they were so discouraged by both the quality and size of what they were seeing. Over and over, I heard the same complaint: "Too much space, too little substance." *The Not So Big House* gave these readers hope that there were alternatives. Perhaps they *could* get a new home with the quality and character of an older one but designed for today's lifestyle.

All too often we are forced to select the most important investment of our lifetime based on a two-dimensional representation—a plan—while those things that really affect our experience of being in a place lie outside the scope of our floor plans and thus go unnamed, and so, unrealized. We long for a sense of shelter and comfort from our homes but tend instead to use words like "spacious" and "expansive" to describe what we think we want. It's no wonder our houses keep getting larger. If we want houses that nurture us, we need to develop a language that describes the qualities of home and not just the quantities. What has drawn so many people to *The Not So Big House* is exactly this: a desire to define these elusive qualities so that the houses they build for themselves will be more than just shelters—they'll be homes.

Creating the Not So Big House broadens the range to include architects from all over the country who are designing homes using Not So Big principles. From the hundreds of submissions I re-

ceived, I've selected 25 beautifully designed houses and remodeling projects that best exemplify Not So Big concepts and provide inspiration for creating your own Not So Big House. The homes are from all over the United States in a rich variety of styles—from a southwestern adobe to a traditional Minnesota farmhouse, a New York apartment to a cottage community in the Pacific Northwest, a jewel in a Chicago suburb to a summer home in Rhode Island.

The plans for most of these homes are available for sale (see p. 258 for details). Unlike grocery-store home plans, each house is illustrated in depth, inside and out, and the ideas that give each house its character and quality are described in detail. The book focuses on ideas and on the qualities that make a home, rather than on size and layout alone. It can help those who want to work with an architect to design a custom home to find the language and ideas to describe their dreams. And those who want a beautifully designed home without taking a custom approach will find plans they can work with.

People are eager for an alternative to the bigger-is-better approach to home design.

What we need are designs of quality, substance, and beauty. *Creating the Not So Big House* is a first step in introducing such designs into the marketplace. Within the coming decade I believe we'll see a whole new

We long for a sense of shelter and comfort from our homes but tend instead to use words like "spacious" and "expansive" to describe what we think we want.

niche in the residential-construction market. It will focus on quality design and construction, using sustainable techniques and materials, and will appeal to buyers who want a home that really nurtures their spirit rather than simply impresses the neighbors with scale. To do this, we have to start with what's important to each of us as we rebalance the way we spend our time, our effort, and our money. It's my hope that this book will give you the tools to create your own Not So Big Home.

The Language of the Not So Big House

THERE'S A TREMENDOUS POWER to naming ideas and concepts. If you have a word for something, you can ask for it, you can think about it, you can agree or disagree with it. But if no one has ever identified the concept, you can only stumble across it accidentally, and even then probably not fully appreciate it. *A Pattern Language*, a book by architect Christopher Alexander and colleagues published in 1977, began the process of naming the concepts that underlie our built environment. It opened my eyes to just how much of what we think of as design is based on hidden patterns that, when understood, can be used to create particular effects.

The home designed by architect Matthew Schoenherr (see "Doing More with Less" on p. 50) includes a wonderful example of one of these hitherto nameless patterns. Matthew took a tiny, one-story summer cottage and remodeled it into a three-story home. On the main level, which was only 500 sq. ft., he placed the entryway, kitchen, dining area, living area, and stairway—all without dividing walls. Surprisingly, the result isn't one big undifferentiated room. Far from it. Each area has its own personality and spatial definition. What separates one space from the next is small and insignificant on the plan—a single 3-ft.-square enclosure that hides the refrigerator from view, with narrow flanking columns on either side. But this one small design element does a tremendous amount of work in defining the "rooms" of the house and in making less do more.

What struck me about this particular feature was that I'd used the same spatial device in my own Not So Big House. By placing the fireplace in the center of the house as a self-contained vertical pod of space, I eliminated almost all of the interior walls while still giving each area its own defined place. Both Matthew and I had used the same highly effective and simple device, yet there is no name for it. Here is a perfect example of a spatial concept that architects use all the time, but that most people don't even know exists. Time for a new term, I thought: a pod of space.

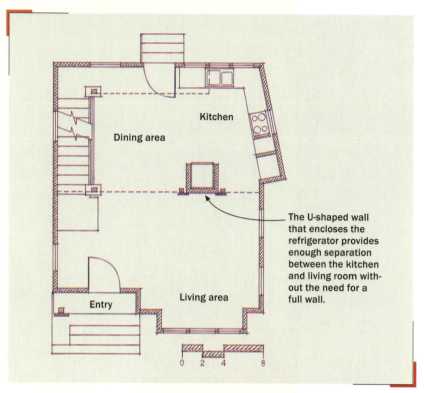

Kitchen

Dining area

Entry

Living area

The U-shaped wall that encloses the refrigerator provides enough separation between the kitchen and living room without the need for a full wall.

0 2 4 8

RIGHT In this small house, the architect used a deceptively simple device to distinguish one activity place from the next: instead of dividing walls, a pod of space hides the refrigerator from view. Its central location allows living, dining, entry, and kitchen areas to be clearly defined places, without blocking sight lines from one space to the next.

Developing a Language of Space and Form

Creating the Not So Big House delves deep into this task of identifying the spatial qualities and concepts that affect us. Using a pod of space is just one of many design concepts I'll explore in this book; others include visual weight, framed openings, spatial layering, and the third dimension (see pp. 11–19). These are not new concepts. Architects have used them for centuries. But although we professionals know how to create these effects, we haven't been successful at explaining the value of what we do to homeowners. By developing a language to help describe the kind of spatial and qualitative experience you want in a house, I hope to bridge this gulf.

Developing a language of space and form is more than just an intellectual exercise. Naming and explaining these design concepts will help you understand what makes spaces work and give you the language to create your own Not So Big House. For example, you'll be able to say, "I want to use *spatial layering* to give the illusion of more space in the living area" or "I like the economy of organizing my master bedroom suite using a *pod of space*." And you, your architect, and your builder will all know what you mean.

In my search for Not So Big Houses to include in this book, I was looking for projects whose architects were focused more on these unnamed spatial concepts than on trendy designs and mere square footage. In selecting the houses, my challenge was to find the best examples. I was looking for houses that were made for today's lifestyles, that were beautifully designed and detailed (but not ostentatious), and that embodied an

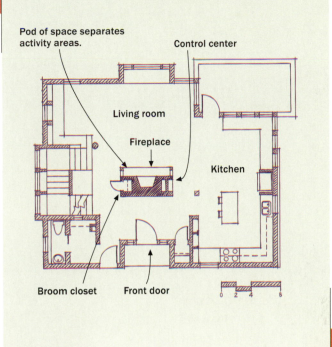

Pod of space separates
activity areas.

Control center

Living room

Fireplace

Kitchen

Broom closet   Front door

0 2 4   8

ABOVE/LEFT In the author's own Not So Big House, a pod of space is used on a slightly larger scale. Here, the pod that separates activity areas contains the control center (visible behind the post), the fireplace, a duct chase, and a broom closet.

LEFT From the living room side, the pod becomes the focal point—wide enough to hide the entryway but narrow enough to allow views to either side into the kitchen and stairway.

attitude of doing more with less. Over a six-month period, I reviewed almost 200 submissions and, from these, selected the 25 outstanding Not So Big Houses you see in this book.

As this portfolio of houses makes clear, the Not So Big approach has nothing to do with a specific style. It can be applied whether you are designing a Pueblo-style adobe (see "Comfort, Pueblo-Style" on p. 114), a traditional Minnesota farmhouse ("A Farmhouse for Our Time," p. 60), or a New England vacation home ("Elegant Simplicity," p. 196). And Not So Big principles are by no means restricted to new construction: They can be implemented whether you are renovating a large but uninviting 1960s split level ("A Sense of

Flow," p. 86) or remodeling a tiny New York apartment ("Tight Quarters," p. 162). These are concepts that transcend style. The common thread among all 25 houses is that they value quality over quantity, comfort over volume, and they are all tailored and personalized to fit the people who live in them.

The Not So Big House Revisited

The inspiration for my first book, *The Not So Big House: A Blueprint for the Way We Really Live,* was a growing awareness that new houses were getting bigger and bigger

OPPOSITE/RIGHT A Not So Big House doesn't necessarily mean small—simply smaller than you thought you needed. Money saved on square footage is spent on quality of design, detailing, and crafting to make a house that's more than the sum of its parts. (PHOTO COURTESY JEREMIAH ECK.)

LEFT Color and form are important features of a Not So Big House, which often includes living space in the roof and tends to be compact rather than sprawling.

BELOW Sometimes Not So Big can be truly tiny, as with these beautifully detailed cottages, with main floors measuring 600–650 sq. ft. Unlike many small homes, these cottages are filled with special touches and fine craftsmanship that make them much more than just little starter houses.

How Big Is Not So Big?

Not So Big doesn't necessarily mean small. It means not as big as you thought you needed. People frequently ask me what is the ideal size for a Not So Big House. The answer depends on your financial situation, the size of your family, and your personal preferences. But as a rule of thumb, a Not So Big House is approximately a third smaller than your original goal but about the same price as your original budget. The magic is that although the house is smaller in square footage, it actually feels much bigger. I'm not advocating that people live in small houses and get used to feeling cramped. A Not So Big House feels more spacious than many of its oversized neighbors because it is space with substance, all of it in use every day.

The Not So Big House: Key Design Concepts

A Not So Big House dispenses with the rooms that are rarely used, so there's money available for the qualities that make a house a home. This is the art of the Not So Big House: to take out square footage that's seldom used, so that you can put the money saved into the detail, craft, and character that will make it eminently comfortable and uniquely yours. In short, it favors quality over quantity. Listed at right are some of the central Not So Big design concepts.

Making one space do two or more things—doing double duty—is a key concept in building Not So Big. Here, a built-in eating area adjacent to the kitchen has been designed to serve both formal and informal occasions, so there's no need for a separate formal dining room.

Shelter around Activity

Creating shelter around a specific activity is a concept that children instinctively understand when they make a cozy hideaway out of a cardboard box. As adults, we do much the same thing when we gravitate to the corner of a room or an alcove to sit. Walls wrap around us so we're protected, but we can look out into the larger space that our sheltered alcove is attached to.

Doing Double Duty

Our homes have grown larger in part to accommodate all the activities we engage in (along with their related furnishings). Rather than building a room for each function, the Not So Big House proposes that we think about ways spaces can be shared. Allowing areas in a house to "moonlight"— making one space serve more than one function—is a way to make them do double duty.

Variety of Ceiling Heights

High ceilings are often considered more desirable than low ones, but high ceilings are often more impressive than comfortable. What's important is not the overall ceiling height; it's the proportion of the ceiling height to the other dimensions of the room that makes it comfortable or not. By varying the ceiling height, spaces are enlivened and individually defined.

Interior Views

Houses are usually designed to take advantage of outside views, with a lot of thought given to getting the windows in just the right places. But we also spend a great deal of time looking within the house, which makes the composition of interior views equally important. If these views are thoughtfully composed, the house becomes beautiful to look at, wherever you are.

Diagonal Views

We know from geometry that the hypotenuse of a right triangle is its longest side. We can use this dimension in home design to increase the perceived size of a house. If you arrange a space so that you can look along the diagonal, from one corner to the opposite one, you are looking along the longest view available, which makes the space feel larger than it actually is.

A Place of One's Own

Our houses are getting bigger in part because we have no place to get away to, no place to be by ourselves. Creating a small area for each adult to make his or her own, just big enough for one, can solve the problem. It can be a place for writing, for painting, for meditating, and for displaying those things that have special personal meaning.

RIGHT This room was originally built with a high vaulted ceiling, but during remodeling it was converted into two rooms, with a new floor platform separating the original living room from the new study above. The reconfigured living room is significantly more comfortable and less echoey than in its preremodeled condition.

but with little redeeming design merit. The sad reality is that once the new homeowners move into these huge, impersonal storage containers, they feel the hollowness of the promise of "bigger is better." Something's missing—all that square footage promises comfort and contentment, but when they move in, it's not there. So they live in the house for only a few years, until they can afford to build another, hoping they can get it right the next time.

Because we equate value with square footage, the same mistake keeps repeating itself. The problem is that comfort has almost nothing to do with how big a space is. It is attained, rather, by tailoring our houses to fit the way we really live and to the scale and proportion of our human form. Judging by the success of *The Not So Big House*, the message is one that resonates with the concerns and aspirations of a lot of people. If you want a home that feeds your spirit, you have to spend more per square foot than you would on the standard suburban starter castle. But spending the same amount of money on a smaller house that's thoughtfully designed and tailored to fit will let you find that something that's missing in all the square footage.

A New Design Language

The Not So Big House explained that the secret to finding a sense of home lies in changing the way we have been taught to think about houses and value—for example, reevaluating the rooms you need in a home, designing a floor plan inspired by today's informal lifestyle, and building to last. The first book also discussed a few of the basic concepts related to the quality of space, such as shelter around activity, interior views, and doing double duty; these central concepts are discussed in the sidebar on p. 10. *Creating the Not So Big House* describes even more concepts that can take the experience of living in a house from mere shelter to the art of dwelling. Let's now look at these key spatial concepts—and give them some names. You'll find many others identified throughout the book.

ABOVE Floor plans are deceptive because they show only two dimensions. When a ceiling height varies, there's nothing on the plan to tell us so. This skylight alcove simply looks like more floor space on the plan, yet in the photo you can see that its character is very different from the rest of the room because of the sloped ceiling and low kneewall.

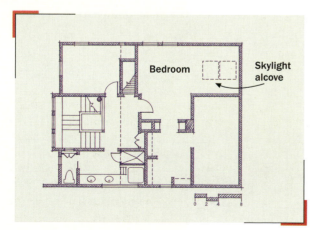

Bedroom   Skylight alcove

The Third Dimension

The key to many of these concepts lies in the third dimension—in the heights of things and how those heights relate to our own human proportions. In *The Not So Big House*, I briefly described the effect that ceiling height has on us. Today, if we want to make a house interesting, the most common response is to raise the ceiling. But a 9-ft.- or 10-ft.-high ceiling can be just as boring as an 8-ft.-high ceiling. It's not so much the height that makes it interesting as the variation in height and the scale of each space in relation to other spaces and to its inhabitants. This three-dimensional experience, combined with the detailing of the interior surfaces, helps to create a comfortable home.

If people really considered the cost of a vaulted ceiling, I'm convinced they would invest their money a different way. The trouble is that it's easy to say "12-ft.-high ceiling" and have someone understand what you mean. It's much harder to communicate a desire for beautiful proportions and comfortable nooks. These things are less tangible and therefore less commonly implemented. Once we have a language for them, I suspect that many more people will choose to spend their money on these life-enhancing qualities rather than on tallness.

Most people think they should be able to tell from a floor plan what a house will look and feel like. But in fact a floor plan tells almost nothing about the "feel" of a house. It's like looking at a map of a city and assuming that it will tell you what it is like to be there. The map represents only two dimensions, while the experience of being in a place resides in three dimensions—in the canopy of the trees, the height of the buildings, the skyways that bridge overhead—everything the map can't show. The only thing a map can tell you is how to direct your feet from one place to another. It's the same with floor plans. The "feel" comes from the experience of our senses, not just from the route we take from one room to the next.

Fear of "Too Smallness"

One of the most important Not So Big concepts is what I call fear of "too smallness." We're so afraid of feeling cramped that we've gone to the opposite extreme and made spaces that are too big to find a place to settle in. Then we have to buy huge furniture to fit the scale of the room. "Oversized" sounds good until you find that you can't touch the floor with your feet. Meanwhile, the cozy corners—often unplanned, leftover spaces—are our favorite spots. It's enjoyable to be able to look into a larger space, but many people prefer the view from the periphery—from a comfortable alcove, for example.

In Matthew Schoenherr's house, you'll see how he's made a space that's only 10 ft. by 12 ft. into a cozy but comfortable living room (see the top photo at right). A room this size would definitely evoke a fear of "too smallness" in many people today. But the space is effective because it offers views into the dining area and kitchen, past the pod of space that gives it visual separation. If it were an enclosed room of that dimension, it would indeed feel small. And if there were no pod of space

Up Close

When you look at a photograph of a small space, it's typical to envision it as larger than it actually is. This is because in order to capture enough of the space in the image, the photographer has to use a wide-angle lens, which tricks the eye into believing the space is larger than it actually is. This photo shows a room that is 10 ft. by 12 ft., but it looks significantly larger. Keep this in mind as you look at the photos throughout the book. If you compare your perception from the photo with the dimensions of the plan, you'll get a better understanding of the true scale.

LEFT Because we're afraid of making spaces too small, we often go to the opposite extreme and make them too big for comfort. The ceiling height in the TV alcove (to the right of the post) is just 6 ft. 10½ in.—too low by most accounts—yet it's the coziest spot in the home. It looks out into the larger spaces that surround it, so it doesn't feel small at all.

The lowered soffit in this bedroom, with its dark wood veneer, gives the ceiling above the bed considerable visual weight. The contrast of this ceiling to the vaulted ceiling beyond helps to define an alcove for the bed in a room that might otherwise feel too tall for a good night's sleep.

BELOW This small house also has a darker ceiling, created by exposing the floor framing of the level above. The color of the wood again gives the entire ceiling a visual weight, which actually makes it seem less tall than it really is. If all the joists were covered with drywall and painted white, the room would appear taller, but it would lose its human-scale proportions in the process.

dividing the activity areas, it would also feel small, because all 500 sq. ft. of the main floor would be perceived as one place, housing five different functions, all on top of one another.

Designing my own home showed me how sensitive I had become to clients' fears of "too smallness." I knew that I wanted a low-ceilinged alcove for reading and watching TV, to contrast with the 8-ft.-high ceilings of the rest of the main level. I made the space just 6 ft. 10½ in. tall, and it's easily my favorite spot to sit. But until I built this house, I'd never even suggested building a ceiling less than 7 ft. tall, because so many people have this fear of feeling cramped. Now that I have an example of such a space to show clients, I've found that many people ask me to duplicate it in their homes. It wouldn't be appropriate for an entire room, but for small alcoves it's in proportion to the activity area, and it feels just right.

Visual Weight

Another technique architects use to manipulate the sense of scale in a space is called visual weight. If a room has a smooth, flat ceiling that's painted a light color, it will feel taller than if it were textured in some way (with exposed beams, for example) and a darker color. The darker and more textured the surface, the heavier it will appear. And heaviness feels lower, because it is more present in our peripheral vision, even when we're not looking directly at it. In the house shown in the photo at left, you'll see that for the size of the room the ceiling is quite tall (about 10 ft.). If the ceiling had been drywalled and painted white to match the walls, it might have felt too tall for the space. But by exposing the floor framing for the level above, the

RIGHT In this little cottage, framed openings are used frequently to indicate room changes without solid walls. Here we see several framed openings—the first used to define the entrance into the kitchen from the living room, the second framing the opening into the eating nook, and a third framing the window and the view beyond.

natural wood color and the texture created by the joists make the ceiling appear heavier and thus lower, in keeping with the proportions of the room.

Framed Openings

Another spatial concept relates to the effect you get by setting off a change of place with a framed opening. Surround an opening with trim, and you subtly communicate this change and, in so doing, give the places on either side their own separate identities. Think about a front door, for example. When you move through the framed opening of the door, you are aware of moving through a gateway that separates exterior from interior. The way you feel once inside is very different from the way you felt outside. The frame informs you that you've entered a new place, and you experience that new place differently as a result.

Although we associate this concept primarily with doorways, it can be employed in any location where you want to distinguish one space from another. For example, in the Third Street Cottage community in Washington State, architect Ross Chapin used this technique to increase the feeling of spaciousness in the tiny cottages (see the photo at right). Wide framed openings between kitchen, living, and dining areas clearly define each activity place within a minimal area.

This technique was used frequently in bungalows of the early 20th century, and for the same reason: to make less space do more. The cased archways of these old gems are one of their most appreciated features. If you've ever been in a bungalow where the archways have been removed between the dining and living areas

ABOVE Spatial layering is a device that architects use to make a space seem larger than it really is. Here, you see through a doorway to a glass screen beyond it, to a column and beam beyond that, and finally to the living room, with its built-in bench and tiny square viewing window. The layers make this distance, and the variety of spaces to explore, seem greater.

to make the space seem more open, you know that the effect is exactly the opposite. The combined room suddenly seems small, not big enough for the two functions that it previously housed quite adequately. The framed opening gives each space its own personality.

In general, the wider the moldings, the more prominent the perception of differentiation will be. One of the most regrettable trends in home design over the past few decades has been the decrease in the size of trim moldings used around windows and doors. Although it is possible to make a big impact with narrow trim, the standard ranch-style casings on the interior and minimal brick-mold casings on the exterior typically make it look as though each window and door has been unceremoniously and gracelessly shoved into the wall. It's analogous to hanging a picture on the wall without a frame. It'll do in a pinch, but it doesn't look good. In many of the houses in this book, you'll see that the exterior trim has been used to give the house a face of sorts and a noticeable personality that defies stylistic designation.

Spatial Layering

The concept of layering takes the idea of framed openings one step further. This technique uses a series of openings and surfaces, implied and otherwise, to subtly break the perceived space into segments. Architects use this concept a lot but have a hard time explaining it. You almost have to see it to understand, but once you do, it can be a powerful tool in making the most of the space you have.

One of the houses in this book beautifully illustrates this concept. Michaela Mahady of SALA Architects used layering in the interior of the Whole Nine Yards house to give the illusion of more space (see p. 244). In the photo on the facing page, you can see four layers defined by three framed openings. The columns with beams above give definition to the walkway that runs through the center of the plan but still allow it to serve as an extension of both the living and dining areas. The glass partition just visible to the left of the first column is like a translucent membrane between two of the layers.

Just as happens with one framed opening between two rooms, layering gives the illusion that each space is larger because it tells the eye where one place stops and the next starts, even though there are no walls to obstruct the view. We interpret this subconsciously as bigger, because we perceive multiple zones. Take away the beams and columns and there's just one not very big, undifferentiated space.

Theme and Variations

One final concept you should keep in mind as you create your own Not So Big House is developing a theme and variations throughout the design. Every house in this book employs this concept, and it's what gives each its integrity and at least some of its personality. If you want a house to have unique characteristics that make it more than just an assemblage of spaces, you can adopt a few special shapes or materials that are repeated throughout

ABOVE The author's own house illustrates a play on a theme and variations, using a form (the circle) and a material (glass block). Above the front door there's a large translucent window in the shape of a partial circle, directly centered below the ridge of the roof. A frame of 12-in. glass blocks accentuates the framed opening around the door.

LEFT As you step inside, you see the circle theme repeated in the curve of the partial wall adjacent to the stairway down to the lower level. As you move into the house and up the stairway to the second floor, the curve continues through the upper-level railing.

the house. If this is done heavy handedly, it will look clunky or will make you think "Enough already." If you've ever seen a house with an octagonal window in almost every room, you'll know what I mean. But when used thoughtfully, a house with a theme and variations is like a well-composed piece of music. From one movement to the next, you know it's the same piece because themes will return as it proceeds, though never repeated exactly as before.

In my own house I used two themes—one a shape (a circle) and the other a material (glass block)—to tie the design together. Looking at the house from the street, the first thing that strikes you is the big round window in the gable end above the garage roof (see the photo at right on p. 17). As you step up to the front door, you notice that the door is framed by large glass blocks that seem to highlight the shape of the door. Once you cross the threshold and look into the house, to the left is a curved wall that extends up the stairs to form the handrail for the upper flight, creating a perfect semicircle as it goes. At the upper landing, the circle theme continues with a barrel-vaulted ceiling above. And if you're observant, you'll notice that the barrel vault continues into the bathroom, where it frames the round window that you saw on the front of the house. As a finishing touch, the circle form is continued on the wall with a mirror cut to the same radius.

RIGHT At the upper landing, the circle form becomes still more apparent. Here, you can see the other side of the translucent front window; the shape is continued with the mirror and the barrel-vaulted ceiling above.

From the backyard, you can see the final expression of the theme. The same curve that was present on the front of the house and that ran though the bathroom and second-floor ceilings extends out to the south wall, where it provides the perimeter trim between the stucco and the shingle patterning. On this rear elevation, you can also see the repetition of the glass block pattern, which now fully frames a perfectly square window that aligns with the front door on the other side of the house.

These are not themes and variations that hit you over the head. They're there, but they play their integrating function quietly, so that most people won't even

be consciously aware of them. That's where the art of the concept lies. You've probably heard the expression, "The whole is greater than the sum of its parts." A Not So Big House is always more than the ingredients that went into it, and it's this weaving of themes, variations, personal touches, and lifestyle patterns that creates a whole that's profoundly satisfying. Architects often hear from their clients that once they move into their own Not So Big House, they don't want to leave, because they've finally found out what home is all about. It's a perfect reflection of who they are and how they live, and it's just big enough to be a perfect fit.

Creating Your Own Not So Big House

The 25 Not So Big Houses you'll see in this book show how spatial concepts like layering and framed openings can be implemented to enhance the livability of today's homes. There's a wide variety of architectural styles represented by these houses, and they come in many different sizes, from 560 sq. ft. at the low end to 3,000 sq. ft. at the high end. There are also several remodelings, demonstrating that a Not So Big House doesn't have to be new to qualify for the title. You can take an older home and, using the concepts described here, transform it into a house in which every space is tailored to your everyday needs and that truly fits the way you live.

The shaping and crafting of space, form, and light is the medium of the architect. It's like the artist's canvas, brush, and palette. Whether or not you plan to use an

LEFT The barrel-vault shape extends all the way through the house to the back elevation, where it is expressed as a graphic design, separating both materials and color areas. In the center of the implied circle is a single glass block. And below it is a frame of glass blocks, like those at the front door, surrounding a square window that aligns exactly with the front entry on the other side.

architect, the ideas in this book will give you a good start in understanding some of the tools of the trade. They have everything to do with the shaping of space. Just remember that we live in a three-dimensional world. It's time to stop hoping that a better floor plan will somehow help us find home. We have to start conversing in the language of the third dimension, making homes that are sculpted to the proportions and harmonics of our own human scale. As you read on, keep your eyes and ears open for these new concepts. They are the tools that will help us make the houses of today into the homes we long to live in.

Inside the
Not So Big House

A Timeless Classic

ABOVE Situating the house and garage at right angles to one another and connecting them with a breezeway creates a view through to the backyard from the driveway and also makes the whole house seem less massive. The entry door, just to the right of the breezeway, serves guests and family alike.

AS I SEARCHED FOR HOUSES ACROSS the country to illustrate the concepts behind building Not So Big, I discovered something I hadn't realized before: It's rare to find an architecturally designed house that doesn't have a vaulted or two-story ceiling somewhere in the design. Although higher ceilings can be dramatic, they add to the structural complexity of the house and thus increase the cost per square foot. And they don't necessarily make the house more livable or more beautiful. Extra money is invested on framing this expansive volume that could have been spent instead on the simple details and proportioning that really add to a home's comfort.

This project from architect Peter Twombly is an example of a house without any tall spaces. It's a very simple structure and form, elegantly detailed with a minimum of fanfare. It's not ostentatious. It's not trying to be clever, unique, or outrageous. It's simply beautiful and comfortable. Let's see how he did it.

Stone lends this unassuming home a timeless quality that defies age.

OPPOSITE The kitchen in this house is a little like the helm of a ship, with a wide pass-through that looks into the dining and living rooms. The posts and beams that provide the structure for the second floor also serve to define the rooms below.

Using a Belt Line

As was common in Shingle-style homes of the early 20th century, this house is banded by a belt line: a wide piece of trim below which all the indents of the main level occur and from which the windows appear to be suspended. A belt line is an excellent graphic device for composing a home's exterior. It organizes the upper and lower sections of the design and provides a graceful transition between materials. The only element that breaks the banding is the chimney, which serves to root the house firmly to its site.

On the front of the house (see the photo on p. 23), the lower section is mostly stone, while shingles are used on the sides, back, and upper section. With a higher budget, the architect might have selected to use stone for the entire lower section. It's not unusual to use a different color, as well as a different material, for the lower and upper areas—a characteristic you'll often see in older homes with a belt line.

If you're planning a belt line on your own home, you might try the following exercise to see what colors you like best: Take a drawing of the front face of the house, and make a number of copies. Then, use crayons or colored pencils to experiment with different colors above and below the belt line. Also, give some thought to the color of the belt line itself. It's typical to use the same color for the belt line as for the trim around windows.

This is a house with a very simple structure and form, elegantly detailed with a minimum of fanfare.

Peter's approach to the design resulted from a fairly limited budget, at least by architect's standards. As with many things of beauty, this economy of means led to a more elegant and satisfying result than an excess of showy details ever could. Think of a haiku. Its power to affect us comes in large part from the constraints imposed by its form, which is so restrictive that every word must transcend the structure. When it does, the effects are deeply moving. So it is with architecture. Peter knew that he would need to make the house very simple to build if it was to stay within budget. So spans were kept short, ceiling heights standard, and the entire structure was designed for conventional framing and lumber sizes.

The house is essentially a rectangular box, with small sections scooped out for the front entry and to either side of the piano alcove to give the front facade some visual interest. The only other

ABOVE Rather than standard spindles, this stair railing is made with 1x4s spaced an inch apart, with a keyhole cutout in every other board. Together with the elegantly proportioned newel post, the stairway looks quite different from the visual approach, yet it is simple and inexpensive to build. It's small touches like this that give a house a personality all its own.

LEFT The exposed rafters and graceful swoop of the roof edge add an artistic touch to the simplicity of the house. It doesn't take a lot to make a significant statement when the rest of the design is so restrained. The tiny hole drilled in the end of the rafter tail provides a subtle theme that's repeated in the stairway railing.

structural embellishment is the addition of a lean-to porch and kitchen eating area, which look out toward a pond to the east. What grows out of these constraints is a surprising amount of spatial complexity and variety.

One Entrance

The clients, Randy and Maggie, were moving from a standard builder's colonial, with an attached garage and a seldom-used formal entry. They assumed that their new house would have the same arrangement. But Peter pointed out that by separating the garage from the house with a breezeway, they could eliminate the garage entry to the house and combine the formal and informal entryways.

When a garage is attached to the house, it's almost inevitable that the family entry is through a laundry or mudroom—hardly an appealing welcome home. Meanwhile, the front foyer is lavished with dollars and pizzazz that are seldom appreciated. Creating a single functional and attractive entrance gives the family the pleasure of entering their home through a well-designed entry every day, and the strategy saves space in the process.

With this newly designed entry, guests and family now enter through the same front door. Just to the left are the mudroom, powder room, and study, making it easy for the kids to drop off their backpacks and for Randy and Maggie to set down their mail and briefcases. The view that greets them is of the window at the far end of the living room, which draws the eye in and acts as an invitation to the living area.

ABOVE Although the kitchen itself has no windows directly to the outside, the breakfast-nook windows provide plenty of light and view. They function like the traditional window over the sink—there just happens to be a usable space in between. (PHOTO COURTESY WARREN JAGGER.)

RIGHT The pass-through allows easy conversation between the cooks and people in the dining and living areas. To keep costs down, the kitchen has laminate countertops and reasonably priced cabinetry. If the composition is well done, you don't need expensive finishes.

All the main living spaces are connected to one another visually, but there's still a strong distinction between one place and the next.

Interior Windows

All the main living spaces are connected to one another visually, but there's still a strong distinction between one place and the next. The kitchen is defined by a wall that separates it from the dining and living areas, but there's a wide pass-through opening that connects the three spaces. Without this framed opening, the house would function very differently. When a space can't be seen, it is typically seldom used. Take away the pass-through, and the living room would be nearly invisible from either kitchen or breakfast nook. To socialize with someone working in the kitchen, you'd have to leave the living room. Most of the living in the house would thus gravitate to the breakfast nook and kitchen, and the living and dining rooms would go largely unused.

ABOVE The breakfast nook is an excellent example of a large alcove. It's a small block of space with a lowered ceiling, filled with light and with views into a larger room beyond. We tend to gravitate to such comfortable corners. (Why else do we find ourselves asking for the corner booth when we go to a restaurant?)

ABOVE Although this home has no vaulted ceilings or two-story spaces, the living room has been given a higher ceiling by dropping the floor two steps down. In this way, the living room is distinguished as the most important space on the main level. Unlike so many vaulted great rooms, however, this space remains eminently comfortable. It takes only a small increase in height to make a big impact.

Such a seemingly insignificant alteration can make a big difference in how one lives in a house. There are many houses, old and new, that could benefit from the implementation of this simple concept. But because we don't have a name for it, we don't know how to ask for it, and so it rarely gets designed. You can think of this visual access between spaces as a "connecting view" or an "interior window." By whatever name, the idea is to keep different activity areas in sight of each other so no room is isolated from the action.

Four Alcoves

Within the nearly symmetrical form of the main-level floor plan, there are four alcoves of varying shapes and sizes. An alcove is essentially a block of space attached to and opening onto a main living space. It houses a peripheral activity, so that more than one thing can be happening at the same time without the activities conflicting.

The largest of these alcoves is the breakfast nook. At 10 ft. 6 in. by 12 ft., it's the perfect size for a small table and chairs. With windows on three sides, it's also filled with light and views. From this cozy space, you can look out into the yard, so there's a sense of expansiveness. And you can also look into the house, through several rooms, so there's a sense of connectedness. This is the kind of space that people tend to be attracted to: a smaller space looking into a larger space. Make it larger and it would lose its appeal. Like a booth at a restaurant, scale is critical to comfort, and bigger is not necessarily better.

There's a second alcove made especially for the grand piano. Place such a piano in the main part of the room and it would dominate the space and add significantly to its formality. But put it in its own alcove, and it takes on a subordinate role. The beauty of its form can still be appreciated, but you don't feel that you're waiting for the concert to begin, as happens when the piano is center stage.

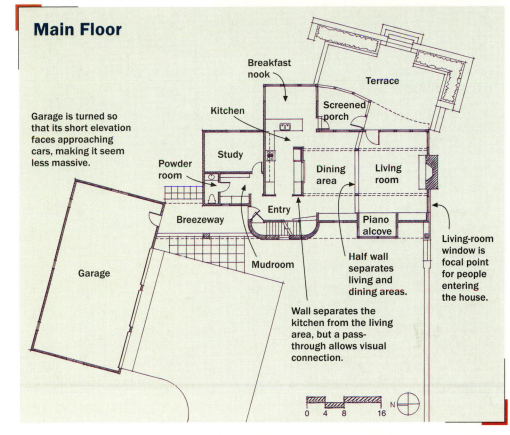

Main Floor

Breakfast nook

Terrace

Garage is turned so that its short elevation faces approaching cars, making it seem less massive.

Kitchen

Screened porch

Study

Powder room

Dining area

Living room

Breezeway

Entry

Piano alcove

Garage

Mudroom

Half wall separates living and dining areas.

Living-room window is focal point for people entering the house.

Wall separates the kitchen from the living area, but a pass-through allows visual connection.

0 4 8   16   N

Architect:
Estes/Twombly Architects, Inc.

Builder:
Gardner Woodwrights

Size: 2,900 sq. ft.

Location:
southern R.I.

Upper Floor

Bathroom

Bedroom

Bedroom

Master bedroom

Guest bedroom

Laundry   Closet   Master bathroom

0 2 4 8

ABOVE Comfort is defined less by the furniture we choose than by the shape of the space, the quality of the light, and the crafting and composition of places for living. This spot by the living-room window, for example, invites you to settle in. It's the combination of chair, light, and alcoves that makes it so appealing. (PHOTO COURTESY WARREN JAGGER.)

The piano alcove is flanked by two smaller alcoves, which house built-ins and display places, creating a depth and variety of space that makes for a visual feast. This is an example of spatial layering. It gives the impression that the outside walls of the house are extra thick and that the alcoves have been scooped out of them to reveal a bit of the world beyond. It's this kind of depth and visual complexity that we've all but lost in new houses today. Instead there's the feeling that everything is paper-thin and could easily be blown away in a high wind.

Rooted to the Ground

The stone used for the front columns, the stairway enclosure, and the chimney adds to the sense of solidity and permanence that is so fundamental to this house. One of the reasons Randy and Maggie bought this particular piece of property was because they liked the old stone walls that ran across it. For them, the walls recalled a time when the area was farmland. In addition to rebuilding some of the existing farm walls, the owners wanted to use some of the stone in the house itself. Although stone is an expensive material to install, by selecting some key areas and locating the house to take advantage of one of the farm walls, a little has been made to go a long way.

Few things speak to us like stone—a simple, strong material created over millennia and solid as the earth. It lends this unassuming home a timeless quality that defies age, and chances are it will still have that quality 200 years from now.

The fireplace surround is made of Rhode Island blue granite with Belgian pavers used instead of regular firebricks, giving it a timeless look and feel. The mantle itself is made of maple, set upon stone brackets. And the sides of the stone-work are battered, or narrowed slightly, echoing the shape of the newel post at the entry. These are subtle moves, but the effect is striking.

LEFT The window in the stairway to the basement is set close to the ground, an intriguing puzzle, perfectly aligned in the center of the wall and directly below the windows above. It's gone from just a window in a wall to an image in a frame, drawing you to take a closer look.

A House
for Today and
Tomorrow

WHEN BETH ASKED ARCHITECT
Murray Silverstein to design a cabin for her on a wooded site in Northern California, she wasn't sure whether she would make it her year-round residence or keep it only for weekend and vacation use. As a single woman, she didn't need a lot of space, but she wanted whatever she built to be beautiful and flexible—a place that felt like a retreat. What evolved is a house with the transformational abilities of a chameleon, despite a deceptively simple floor plan.

In order to appreciate this home's flexibility, we need to go back to Beth's original vision. She is a therapist by profession and was considering the possibility of living in the house year-round and also having her office there. She wanted a space that was professional and private, with a separate entrance so clients wouldn't have to walk through her living area in order to reach the office. In-home consulting practices come with their own special challenges. They need acousti-

A house designed to accommodate a variety of possible future living arrangements can actually benefit from the constraints imposed upon it.

cal privacy and a quality of quiet removal from the activities of the rest of the house, so that clients won't be uncomfortable talking openly. They also require ready access to a powder room, preferably one not in view of the living space.

These are, of course, the same qualities you find in a comfortable bedroom. To accommodate the restrictions of her budget and the small scale Beth was seeking, Murray realized that he could make that private realm do double duty. So he designed the second level to be divisible into two rooms—an office/study and a bedroom beyond. By nestling the house into the side of the hill to the northwest, he created an entry for clients halfway between the main and upper levels, allowing them to enter without ever encountering the main living space. The compact powder room on the landing could serve both the office and the bedroom. Meanwhile, family and friends enter directly through the solarium porch at the end of the beautiful flagstone path connecting house and driveway. Although Beth hasn't yet used the work-at-home option, her house is ideally set up for such an arrangement.

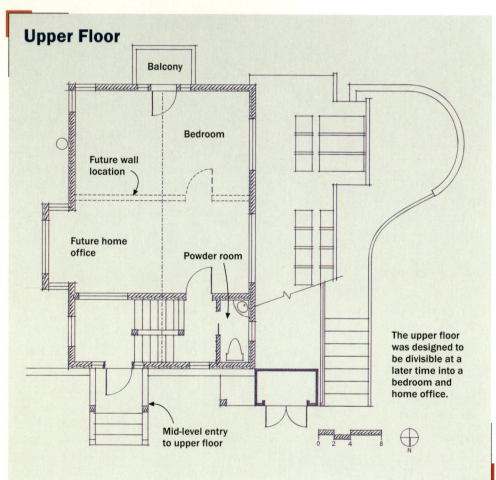

Upper Floor

Balcony

Bedroom

Future wall location

Future home office

Powder room

The upper floor was designed to be divisible at a later time into a bedroom and home office.

Mid-level entry to upper floor

0 2 4 8

N

ABOVE With its steeply sloped roof and 5-ft.-high side wall, this bedroom feels both cozy and spacious. If the wall were raised to 8 ft., however, the room would take on the proportions of a cathedral—not a comfortable place for sleeping. Every dimension in our homes should relate to human scale. Taller doesn't automatically mean better.

Architect: Jacobson Silverstein Winslow Achitects

Builder: Axel Nelson, General Contractor

Size: 1,150 sq. ft.

Location: Inverness, Calif.

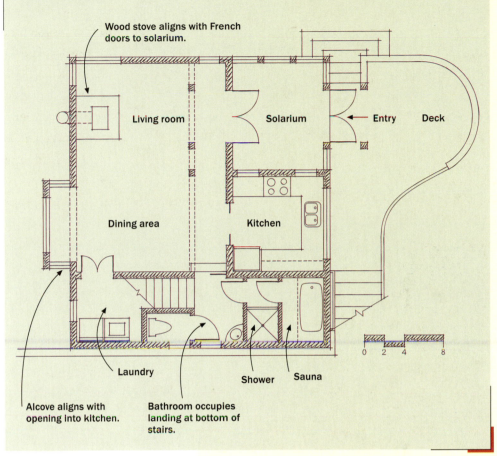

Main Floor

Wood stove aligns with French doors to solarium.

Living room

Solarium

Entry

Deck

Dining area

Kitchen

Laundry

Shower

Sauna

Alcove aligns with opening into kitchen.

Bathroom occupies landing at bottom of stairs.

0 2 4 8

Guest Suite with a Twist

Since Beth planned to have guests every once in a while but didn't want to have a room devoted to this purpose alone, she was willing to combine two functions that are an unusual pairing. The solarium porch is used primarily as an entryway, but when friends are visiting, it doubles as the guest sleeping area. Although in most houses an entry is one of the most public spaces in the house, in this home it can be turned into a very private space, thanks to the existence of the mid-level entry. The exterior doors are locked, the French doors into the living space covered with drapes, and the transformation is complete. Now it's a guest room or away room.

The One-Bath House

But what about a bathroom for the guests? When there's a bedroom on each level, it's a foregone conclusion these days that you must include a full bathroom on each level as well. Bathrooms are expensive, though, and guest bathrooms are typically seldom used. So Murray came up with a clever solution—one bathing area to serve both levels. The landing at the bottom of the stair-

Although in most houses an entry is one of the most public spaces in the house, in this home it can be turned into a very private space.

case is in fact also the main bathroom. A sliding door and two steps up separate it from the main-level living space. Directly across from the stair is the door into the shower. A door beyond that leads into the tub room. Lower the lid over the tub, and the room is transformed into a sauna. To the left of the stair is the toilet, in its own tiny room under the staircase to the upper level. And on the landing itself is the sink, tucked into a corner beside the window. Although this may seem a strange way to accommodate a bathroom, if every cubic inch must be used effectively, any space is fair game.

Defining Places

The rest of the main level is classic Not So Big in arrangement, with a single dining and living area and a kitchen that's open to both. When a formal dinner is in progress, Beth can close off the kitchen from view with sliding doors, but most of the time they remain open. The dining table has its own small alcove, just 7 ft. wide. The beams above it serve to mark off the space and give it a sense of enclosure, without lowering the ceiling or blocking the windows.

Often, in an effort to accommodate chair movement, dining spaces are made overly large and their intimacy is lost. Here, the space fits perfectly with the proportions of the house, and the table has become a favorite spot to sit. Without the alcove, though, the house would feel very different. There'd be no sheltered place to go to and no relief from the rectangular form of the room. Even when money is limited, including a small alcove like this one adds a spatial vitality that's well worth the expense.

ABOVE Placing a window at the end of a walkway draws you toward it. Remove the window and you'll be much less inclined to move in that direction. The two steps are part of the flight to the second floor and lead to the main-level bathroom. The landing houses the bathroom sink, tucked around the corner to the left.

RIGHT You pass through the shower area to reach the tub beyond, which is in its own cocoon-like room. When the lid is folded down to cover the tub, the room turns into a sauna. One space serves two functions, with a minimum of fuss, proving that a little creativity can save a lot of square footage.

When in Doubt, Line It Up

Another aspect of organizing space is used here that doesn't add any cost, yet is rarely implemented. Look at the floor plan on p. 35 and you can see that the dining alcove is perfectly aligned with the opening into the kitchen. The same is true of the wood stove, which is directly across from the French doors to the solarium. Aligning views and features in this way gives the whole house an integrity that's palpable. It's not something you will stop and take note of every day—in fact very few people will consciously observe such alignments. But the place will feel good, as though all is right with the world. Someone has taken the time to make a harmonious composition, and we appreciate it instinctively, even when we don't realize why.

Another ordering device used on the main level to add both character and comfort is the heavy timber walkway that leads from the entryway to the staircase. Although this area is still very much a part of the main living

TOP Why hide away the beautiful objects you own? Here, a collection of ceramics becomes the wallpaper for the living room. These mugs and plates are used every day and, when not in service, stored in this specially designed rack adjacent to the kitchen.

RIGHT An alcove creates a sense of shelter around the activity it houses. Although many alcoves have a lowered ceiling, here it is implied rather than actual, with the trim line between windows transforming into a beam that bridges the space. A ceiling doesn't have to be solid to create enclosure.

Shibui

*I*n Japanese, the word *Shibui* is used to describe a quality of design that many Not So Big Houses possess. It can be an elusive concept to grasp, however, because we have no comparable word in our language. Words that combine to give a sense of its meaning include simplicity, elegance, beauty, functionality, restraint, reserve, refinement, and quietude. The term can apply to anything that has been designed, from an article of clothing to a piece of furniture to a building.

But none of these words describes how this quality comes into being. Though something *Shibui* looks effortlessly simple, even inevitable, it takes much labor and refinement to make it so. The quality of *Shibui* evolves out of a process of complexity, though none of this complexity shows in the result.

Shibui often seems to arise when an architect is striving to meet a particular design challenge. When you stop to think back on houses that have made an impact on you, they'll often be the ones where an awkward problem has been cleverly solved in a way that makes you think, "Well, of course! How else could it be?" When something has been designed really well, like the house shown here, it has an understated, effortless beauty, and it really works. It's simply *Shibui*.

It takes real skill to create an intimate small house that satisfies a complicated set of requirements—and does so without feeling confined.

space, it's also separated from it by the line of columns, lowered ceiling sections, and supporting beams. It's a little like the arcades you see in Europe, along centuries-old shopping streets. The kitchen and solarium are the shops, the main living area is the open-air plaza, and the walkway—the arcade—offers shelter as people come and go. There's a sense of order and layering about the arrangement that makes us comfortable because it helps us subconsciously understand what's going on: This is the path to get from one place to the next. And it's no accident that the windows at either end of the walkway are lined up along its central axis.

This little house has proportions that optimize comfort. Architects will be the first to admit that, although you can have fun designing a larger house with few constraints, it takes real skill to create an intimate small house that satisfies a complicated set of requirements—and does so without feeling confined. A house like this one, designed to accommodate a variety of possible future living arrangements, can actually benefit from the constraints imposed upon it.

The house has gone on to gracefully accommodate some unexpected new uses over the years. It's recently become a much-loved weekend home, not only for Beth but also for her new husband and baby. It illustrates well how a little forethought can extend the usefulness of a house as opportunities and lifestyle choices change without compromising its originally intended function—a quiet forest getaway for one. A house designed as beautifully and thoughtfully as this one can take on all manner of lifestyle changes—even the unpredictable ones.

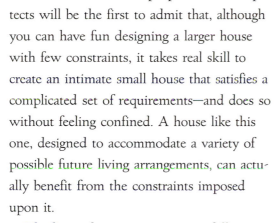

BELOW **As you enter the main living area from the solarium, visible here through the French doors, you emerge under the lowered timber walkway. The experience of entering is accentuated by the contrast between ceiling heights, which creates the experience of compression followed by release.**

The Essence of Home

I N SELECTING NOT SO BIG HOUSES
for this book, I looked for dwellings that have an archetypal
quality—houses that resonate with the deep-rooted vision of
home that many people carry within their hearts and minds.
Features of this archetype include a
steep, single-gabled roof, usually with
one or more dormers; a centrally located entry with its own sheltering
roof; and a massive chimney, either at
the center of the house or at one or
both ends. These basic features, combined with pleasing proportions and
a well-chosen site, speak to us of
home. Not surprisingly, as we look
back through the history of the
house, we find dwellings from many
cultures that have this same general form. Architects refer to this
as "vernacular architecture"—literally, architecture that has grown
from the native building patterns of a culture.

*The house embodies in its
exterior form much of what
we long for today—a house
that says Home before you
ever step through the door.*

ABOVE A small sitting balcony is
aligned with the top of the stairs and
the middle dormer of the house—the
exact center of the floor plan. The combination of natural-wood newel posts
and handrails with white painted,
closely spaced spindles is a reference
to classic detailing and proportioning.

OPPOSITE Based on images from the
past but with a contemporary twist, this
house is almost symmetrical but not
quite. With its darker base, white
second-story dormers, bold green roof,
and central chimney, it is distinctive but
familiar. It resonates with the arche-
types that say Home. (PHOTO COURTESY
JEREMIAH ECK.)

The windows throughout the main level are larger than normal, with a fixed upper transom set above out-swinging casements. The combination gives the look of an old-fashioned double-hung window, where the upper section was often shorter than the lower one. The raised platform of the window bay offers a comfortable place for overflow seating during parties and larger gatherings.

There is one house in particular that has spoken to many people in this way over the last few years. In my own architectural practice, clients would frequently bring in magazine photos of this house (first published in *Fine Homebuilding* magazine in 1990) and tell me how much they liked the look of the exterior. It was something they instinctively responded to without being able to say why. Designed by architect Jeremiah Eck for a couple who were building on land that their family had owned for generations, it embodies in its exterior form much of what we long for today—a house that says Home before you ever step through the door.

What Steve and Nancy were looking for was a modern version of an English cottage. Jeremiah drew from his knowledge of vernacular architecture and historical house forms to develop a design that would fit the needs of the couple and their two young children and reflect their love of the archetypal cottage. With its triple gables, steeply pitched roof, and massive brick chimney, it is an amalgam of imagery found throughout Europe, while also incorporating aspects of the American Gothic.

Building Character

The house is set at the edge of a wood that looks out toward the ancestral family home, across acres of meadowland. Like many other distinctive Not So Big Houses, it seems to have a face, with the two symmetrical gables like a pair of spectacles resting on the bridge of the nose—the third gable. As is typical of many American Gothic homes, the upper section (above the belt line) is made of wide wooden panels with vertical

The Effects of Color

The color of a house can make a dramatic difference in how it looks and feels, but it's rare that we have the opportunity to see what a house looks like in two different color schemes. Thanks to the fact that Steve is a house painter and likes to experiment on his own house, we can see here the dramatic difference between the house as originally painted and how it looks today. When the house was new, Steve left the lower section a natural cedar color, stained with a semitransparent stain. Many people love this natural look, but it requires significant maintenance, with a reapplication of stain every two to three years.

Now Steve has applied a new coat of paint to both upper and lower sections, and the colors give the house a more playful appearance. Where in the original scheme the entire upper section was painted bright white, in the new version the trimwork remains white but the plywood and batten strips are a contrasting blue. In the lower section, the yellow of the siding contrasts only slightly with the trim, and since they are close in color to one another, the eye is drawn to the upper part of the house as the dominant form.

Color is a very personal issue, and one that can elicit some spirited debate among couples. Some people like the whole house to be the same color, while others prefer a darker base and lighter upper section, and still others like it the other way around. But the wonderful thing about color is that it's a relatively easy thing to change. And with the advent of computer-aided design and color modeling, we're able to see the effects of color choices *before* the paint is applied.

(PHOTO TOP RIGHT COURTESY JEREMIAH ECK.)

Upper Floor

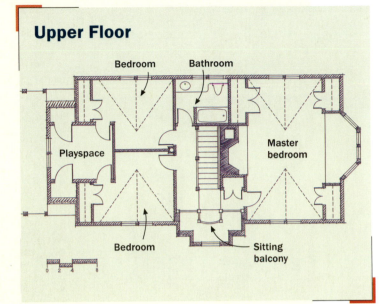

Bedroom

Bathroom

Playspace

Master bedroom

Bedroom

Sitting balcony

0 2 4 8

Main Floor

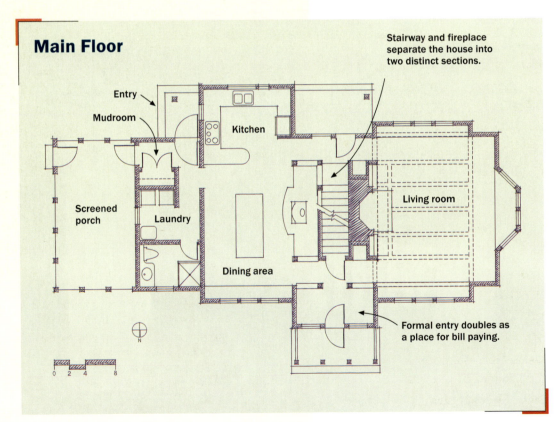

Stairway and fireplace separate the house into two distinct sections.

Entry

Mudroom

Kitchen

Screened porch

Laundry

Living room

Dining area

Formal entry doubles as a place for bill paying.

N

0 2 4 8

batten strips, while the lower section has horizontal lap siding in a contrasting color.

This configuration serves to distinguish one section of the house from another. When we can identify an order to the parts of a design (in this case, main level, upper level, and roof), it gives us a sense of understanding—just as we use commas to break a sentence into phrases so we can take in the content more easily. Remove the commas and you might have to read the sentence a few times to understand what's being communicated. In the same way, if all the exterior surfaces of this house were of the same material and color, it would seem more monumental and, as a result, less inviting.

The trim width around doors and windows is important, too. In most houses today the only trim around windows is the brick mold, a narrow molding that comes with the window. The window looks almost frameless, as if it had been rather unceremoniously shoved into the wall. (Just visit any subdivision built in the last two decades and you'll see what I mean.) In this house, as in most Not So Big Houses, careful attention has been given to each window's framing. Most of the win-

Architect:
Jeremiah Eck Architects, Inc.
Builder:
Jarrett Vaughn Construction
Size: 1,750 sq. ft.
Location:
Holicong, Pa.

Small details combine to give the house a solidity and substance that would otherwise be lacking.

dows have a 3½-in.-wide piece of trim at either side and a deeper, 5½-in. board below the sill. In the case of the two triple-window sets on the main level, they are "hung" from the belt line, which serves as the head trim.

The double-hung windows in the twin gables are surrounded by more dramatic frames, again reminiscent of the American Gothic style. Here, the wide top casing is banded with an additional molding that extends about a quarter of the way down each side, further accentuating the windows' resemblance to eyes. All these small details may seem minor, but they combine to give the house a solidity and substance that would otherwise be lacking. They are characteristic of a house in which the available money has been spent on quality rather than quantity. It's the details that really make it sing.

Table at the Center

Inside, the house continues its interpretation of the past with a floor plan separated into two sections by the stairway and fireplace, a classic layout in many early American houses. Until the invention of extractor fans, the kitchen was often built either in an isolated lean-to structure or in a separate building, to keep the smells of cooking away from the living

ABOVE Without the half wall and columns, this spot by the wood stove would be an unsettling place to sit—at the bottom of the stairs and adjacent to the walkway through to the living room. But with them, this chair has a sense of shelter around it, making it more inviting and comfortable.

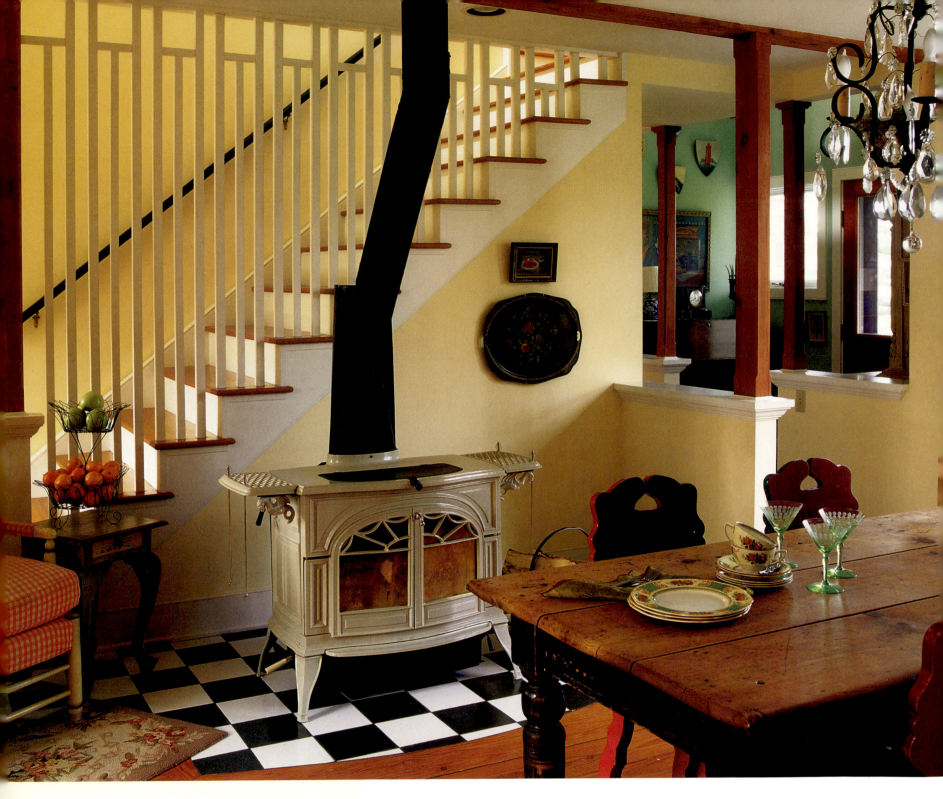

ABOVE The railing between the dining area and the staircase is transparent enough to allow an unobstructed view but solid enough to create a psychological separation. It's an implied wall—more like a lattice than a wall. It gives the stair a sense of enclosure while adding a wonderfully decorative backdrop to the room.

areas of the home. Since modern technology has eliminated this concern, Jeremiah has kept the lean-to form but opened up the kitchen to the dining area, creating one big room with the table as its focus.

When you consider the design of a home, it's important to look at family social patterns and recognize where people tend to gather. For many, the kitchen table is the place. It is only convention that encourages us to make it small and place it in a corner. If the room has an easy comfort like this one, the table can be large and centered in the room without it feeling formal. A table of this kind can still do double duty for both formal and informal occasions, but if it receives an extra nick or two from everyday wear and tear, it's not something you'll lose sleep over.

Just as in farmhouses of the past, the kitchen table is where the family congregates, and its central position puts it at the heart of activity. Adjacent to the wood stove, and with a clear view to the comings and goings of the stairway, it makes the dining area a place that feels vibrant and alive.

An Old-Fashioned Living Room

By contrast, the living room, which in this house is separate from the kitchen, is the quiet place of retreat for the adults. Although most Not So Big Houses have their kitchen, living, and dining areas open to one another, if you like to move into another room after a meal, then that's how you should plan your house. As always, build for the way *you* live.

LEFT This house is full of personal touches that continue the theme of making new out of old. Here, an antique pediment perches above the window like a hat, and a charming old kitchen cabinet hangs above the stove, giving a little more storage and a lot more character to the simple kitchen.

Up Close

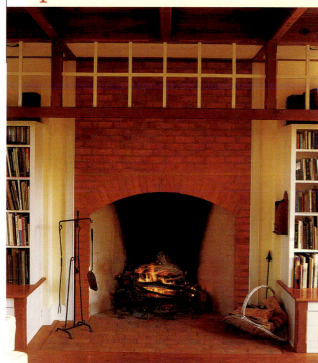

In this home, the fireplace is an important social gathering spot that clearly sees frequent use. Together with the lattice frame above and bookshelves on either side, the whole ensemble suggests an old-world inglenook. But, as with so much else in this house, it's a contemporary version.

RIGHT Since the formal front entry in this house is rarely used (most guests and family arrive by the back door), it has been designed to do double duty as a place for paying bills. The antique desk looks like an appropriate piece for a foyer, but it can fold out into a desk when needed.

BELOW The comfortably furnished living room, centered around an old-fashioned hearth, is intended as the adults' realm for reading and after-dinner conversation. It is more separate from the kitchen and dining area than in many Not So Big Houses, doubling as a quiet away room. (PHOTO COURTESY JEREMIAH ECK.)

For Steve and Nancy, this adult realm of the house was an important and desirable feature that they knew they would use. They like to light a fire on winter evenings and to read and talk after dinner in a more elegant setting than the kitchen allows. By lowering the floor two steps and exposing the beams and flooring of the level above, Jeremiah has made the room almost 2 ft. taller than the rest of the main level, giving it greater visual and spatial weight. The warmth of the wood ceiling, the well-used fireplace, and the comfortable furnishings give it a very different feel than the typical formal living room. Like the exterior of the house, this room says Home.

The Personal Touch

Allowing your house to become a truly personal expression is one of the basic tenets of building Not So Big, and Steve and Nancy have missed no opportunity to give every nook and cranny of their home a colorful, lighthearted quality with the treasures they've collected over the years. There are small collections of special objects here and there, like the array of flower-patterned plates around the mirror at the bottom of the stairs and the coats of arms above the desk in the front-entry niche. There are also a number of "found" architectural objects dotted around, such as the wooden pediment above the kitchen window and the metal screen behind the bed in the master bedroom, which provides some psychological privacy without blocking the view. Often a house that's playfully composed encourages its inhabitants to continue in that same spirit, personalizing wherever they can, and giving the whole house an unselfconscious, friendly feel.

Finding someone to help you design a house that really expresses who you are can be enormously rewarding. It's as though the house both focuses and reflects the way you feel about life, to yourself and to others. So many people today live in houses that, they'll readily admit, don't really fit their spirits. A house like this one is made for the way its owners live and also expresses something more about their values and their delights. A house that's designed specifically for you and your family can enhance your life in a truly remarkable way. Until you've tried it, many houses will *seem* to satisfy, but after living in one that's really "you," you'll understand what coming home is all about.

BELOW A screen made of wrought-iron filigree separates the bed from the window bay. It shelters the head of the bed and still allows views through to the meadows and trees beyond.

A house that's designed specifically for you and your family can enhance your life in a truly remarkable way.

Doing More with Less

No ONE BUT AN ARCHITECT WOULD have dared to try to make the old summer rental cottage in Branford, Connecticut, into a year-round home for a family of four. But Matthew, who has his own architectural practice, and his wife, Beth, an interior designer, were undeterred by the diminutive size of the lot (less than a tenth of an acre) and the tiny footprint of the cottage. In fact, they used the 20-ft. by 24-ft. foundation of the original structure as their starting point and, with the addition of only two small bump-outs to the footprint, made a house that looks inviting on the outside and exudes charm and innovation within.

The house now has three stories and a basement instead of one story and a cellar, and every cubic inch of space is used every day. With only 500 sq. ft. on the main level, Matthew and Beth had to use all their combined inventiveness to make a place that is comfortable for a family to live in without feeling claustrophobic. The house is built vertically instead of horizontally, which is

The house utilizes the principles of building Not So Big to make a little space feel much bigger than it really is.

like thinking outside the box by prying the lid off. It takes this unusual configuration of space and the principles of building Not So Big to make a little space feel much bigger than it really is.

By using the basement level as a playspace for the children and by placing their own bedroom and the children's bedroom on two separate upper floors, Matthew and Beth have created 1,700 sq. ft. of living space. Each level is a treasure trove of clever ideas to make less do more. Most remarkable of all, this is done not through a minimalist approach but with a profusion of personal items, collections, and comfortable furniture.

ABOVE A pleasing graphic composition, the rear elevation is as thoughtfully designed as the front. The bright red door hints at the surprises inside.

RIGHT Unexpected materials are used throughout the house, like the oar instead of a standard handrail and the corrugated metal roofing as wall covering at the front entry. Overcome habitual thinking about how things are supposed to be used, and there's no limit to creativity.

What the Floor Plan Doesn't Reveal

In plan, the main level looks pretty stark—just an oddly formed square with a single U-shaped wall in the middle, which houses the refrigerator. If you were to see this floor plan in a house-plan magazine, you'd probably skip right over it. But this house illustrates the limitations of the floor plan as a device for gauging character. What you can't see in two dimensions is what makes this home such a delight.

The U-shaped refrigerator wall is a small item in the plan, but what it does three-dimensionally is very important. Essentially, the main level needs to accommodate five functions: entering, sitting, cooking, eating, and going up- or downstairs. If walls were added to partition the space according to function, every room would seem very small. But if the space is left completely open, there is little distinction between

Each level is a treasure trove of clever ideas to make less do more.

Architect:
Z:Architecture

Builders:
Matthew Schoenherr,
Michael Fuller

Size: 1,700 sq. ft.

Location:
Branford, Conn.

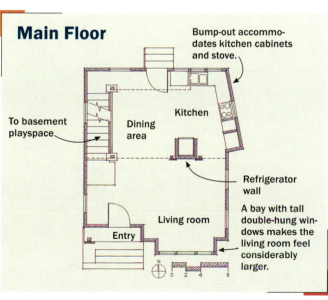

Main Floor

Bump-out accommodates kitchen cabinets and stove.

Kitchen

To basement playspace

Dining area

Refrigerator wall

Living room

Entry

A bay with tall double-hung windows makes the living room feel considerably larger.

Second Floor

Children's bathroom

Master bathroom

Master bedroom

Closets

Beams and a lowered ceiling over the bed add spatial complexity to a room that appears simple in plan.

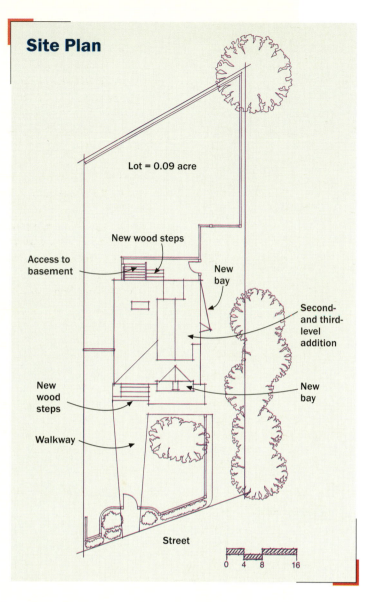

Lot = 0.09 acre

New wood steps

Access to basement

New bay

Second- and third- level addition

New wood steps

New bay

Walkway

Street

0 4 8 16

one area and another, and this also makes a space feel small. The refrigerator enclosure helps to break up the space by providing a separation between the kitchen and the living room, which partially obscures views from one to the other without the complete enclosure of a full wall. It's what I call a pod of space.

The refrigerator pod also serves as a large column. It aligns with the center of the front bay, giving the living room a feeling of symmetry. And finally, from the dining area, it identifies the right-hand edge of the kitchen. Combined with the lowered ceiling over the kitchen and dining area, the four main quadrants of the floor plan are all defined by this simple 36-in. square. Quite an accomplishment for one small box!

Ceiling Magic

On the second level, the master bedroom looks like a regular rectangular room on the plan, but in the photo on p. 57 you'll see that the space itself gives a very different impression. The ceiling is full of unexpected detail, which derives from the structure required to support the kids' room above. There are parallel beams and a lower paneled ceiling over the bed that aligns with the window bay. And the west end of the room is vaulted, following the lines of the roof above. Though not a large area, it provides a high wall surface for Beth's collection of dinner plates (antique and otherwise) and lends a spatial complexity that is quite invisible in the floor plan.

In the kids' upper garret there are more surprises, including a closet that in plan looks perfectly ordinary but which in elevation provides food for some serious head scratching (see the photo on p. 59). The two doors into the closet have transom windows above them, which trick the eye into believing that the doors lead outside.

This house illustrates the limitations of the floor plan as a device for gauging character. What you can't see in two dimensions is what makes this home such a delight.

LEFT The refrigerator is concealed behind this narrow wall, which is the only interior wall on the main level. The flanking columns, made of steel channel concealed behind 1x8 trim, help support the floors above. The opening between kitchen and living room is just wide enough to allow easy communication between the two spaces but narrow enough to screen the sink area from view.

ABOVE When a room is bright, it feels more spacious. The bay window in the tiny 10-ft. by 12-ft. living room makes the space seem significantly larger, thanks to the flood of south light and tall double-hung windows. The bay acts like a light box, bouncing sunlight off the side walls and deep into the room.

RIGHT When the original house was built, money was tight, and the couple had resigned themselves to living with plywood floors for a while. But then Beth had an idea. Why not use wallpaper? This image shows their first wallpaper floor covering, which lasted about three years. (Photo © Candace Tetmeyer.)

The bedroom is topped off with a vaulted ceiling painted with golden stars, which at night gives the distinct impression that the room is open to the sky. It is, in many ways, a magical space.

A Tower of Alcoves

The 2-ft.-deep bay added to the front of the house is another strategy that adds lots of character with minimal means. On the exterior, the two-story structure is painted and detailed to look almost like a tower (see the photo on p. 50). It is distinguished from the rest of the shingled exterior with white clapboard siding and houses all the street-facing windows. Its effect on the interior is even more pronounced, creating alcoves in both the living room and master bedroom, which combine with the windows to work like light boxes. Sunlight bounces off the side walls and into the room, and the light-filled space creates a wonderful illusion of expansiveness. Although the square footage added to each room is minimal—16 sq. ft.—the effect on the perceptible scale of each room is dramatic.

Wallpaper Where?

If you're wondering what the material is on the kitchen and dining-area floors, you're not alone. When I first received snapshots of the house from Matthew and Beth, I called with that very question. I'd never seen anything quite like it. The answer? Wallpaper. Architects don't usually like wallpaper even on walls (we're a purist bunch), but on the floor?

LEFT The master bedroom has a bay identical to the living room's, but here the effect is to define a separate space, delineated by the beams in the ceiling and the paneling over the bed. These are the kinds of details that don't show up in a floor plan but make an enormous difference in how a room functions and feels.

Up Close

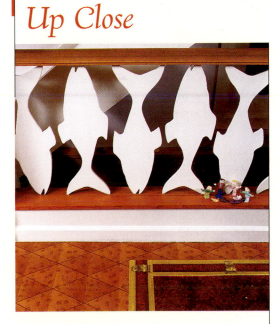

The fish handrail and wallpaper floor are two of the innovative ways the owners personalized their home. There is even a wallpaper rug below the dining table, made by using a room border for the edge and a different paper for the center. The wallpaper is applied just as on a wall, with two coats of polyurethane added once it's down to give some protection to the surface.

When they first finished remodeling the house, having done most of the work themselves, they simply had no money left for floor coverings. Matthew had reconciled himself to the fact that they would have to live with the plywood underlayment for a while. But Beth had a better idea. Although it would last for only a year or two, she suggested laying down wallpaper, adding a urethane finish, and calling it good for the time being. As an interior designer, she loves to make frequent changes to her home anyway.

ABOVE Displaying family history and memories creates a connection back through time and helps children to build a sense of continuity and belonging. In this house, the walls along the stairway to the children's bedroom make a perfect gallery for family photos.

The wallpaper floor was like a license to redecorate. The first wallpaper floor lasted three years, and they liked it so much that they put in another, which gives the house a completely different look and feel.

For innovators like Matthew and Beth, the canvas that their house provides will in all likelihood be a constantly changing, very personal masterpiece for many decades to come. If, like them, you let your imagination roam, and don't let keeping up with the Joneses bother you too much, you can make a house that's packed with ideas, full of fun, and a pleasure to live in. And in most cases, the size has nothing to do with its success.

ABOVE Most kids prefer to sleep in the upper bunk, but in this house there's an even bigger attraction than simply being on top of the world. The large, round window offers views to Long Island Sound, turning this bunk into a window seat as well as a place to sleep.

LEFT The inventiveness in this house extends to optical illusion. Looking at the transom windows above the two doors, you assume that the doors themselves lead outside. But in fact they provide the access to the children's closets. The closet roof aligns with the door headers, so there's enclosed space below.

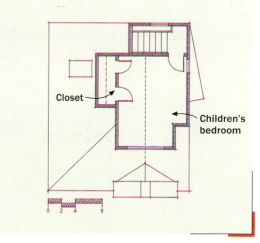

Third Floor

Closet

Children's bedroom

0 2 4 8

A Farmhouse for Our Time

WHILE MANY OF THE NOT SO BIG Houses being built around the country today are modern in style and spirit, there's nothing to say that you can't apply the same concepts to traditional house forms. This Minnesota farmhouse is a perfect example. When architect Jean Larson asked clients Susan and David to bring in pictures that illustrated the look and feel they wanted for their new house, what they came up with had a definite, traditional theme. They clearly liked simple, clean lines—almost spartan, some might say—and were attracted to the classic forms of Midwestern farmhouses. Since their land was in the midst of farm country, Jean felt that this was a good starting point for the design.

This house is reminiscent of the farmhouses of the past but designed for a more contemporary lifestyle.

Many classic farmhouses from the turn of the last century have an L-shaped plan, with four main rooms: kitchen, dining room, living room, and parlor, each occupying one quadrant, with a mudroom/rear entry added on to one side. A wraparound

OPPOSITE A section of the wraparound porch is screened in to serve as an outdoor room in summer. As in classic farmhouses, the roof slope of the porch and other lean-tos is very shallow (only 4-in-12), while the main gable roofs are much steeper (12-in-12).

61

Main Floor

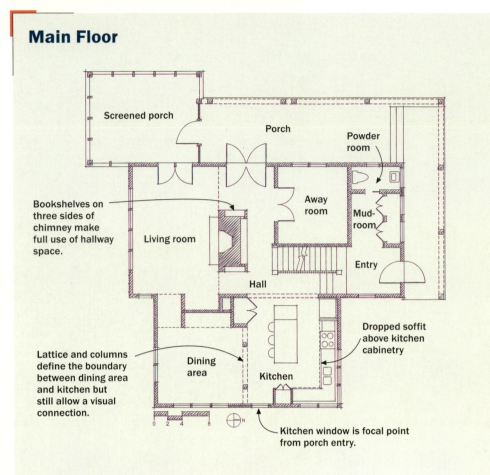

Screened porch

Porch

Powder room

Bookshelves on three sides of chimney make full use of hallway space.

Away room

Mud-room

Living room

Entry

Hall

Lattice and columns define the boundary between dining area and kitchen but still allow a visual connection.

Dining area

Kitchen

Dropped soffit above kitchen cabinetry

0 2 4 8

N

Kitchen window is focal point from porch entry.

porch completes the floor plan. Susan and David wanted a house that was more open than this classic plan, but they still liked the idea of identifiable rooms. The result is a house reminiscent of the farmhouses of the past but designed for a more contemporary lifestyle. Rooms are more open to one another, and views connecting one space to the next have been widened, but the classic farmhouse plan is still very much apparent.

Back-Door Living

In updating the plan for today's lifestyle, Jean reasoned that out in the country nearly everyone comes to the back door, while the formal front door remains largely unused. So, why not make the back door the acknowledged main entry and allow the location that would have been the front door to be the main access to the wraparound porch instead? The strategy works perfectly. Friends and family alike enter through the same doorway, with the garage set a short distance away, just off the knoll of the hill. Meanwhile, the double doors onto the porch extend the living space of the home's interior out into the surrounding landscape.

LEFT When part of a room is bathed in sunlight, our eye tells us there's more around the corner, and we want to go and explore. Without the windows, though, it's not nearly as enticing.

Rooms are more open to one another, and views connecting one space to the next have been widened, but the classic farmhouse plan is still very much apparent.

BELOW The lattice separating the living room from the entrance to the away room completes the rectangle of the room without enclosing it with a solid wall. This makes the room feel bigger but preserves the formal proportions of the room. In summer, the French doors can be thrown wide open to connect indoors and out.

Pathways and Implied Walls

The plan has two central pathways that channel both view and movement and separate the four rooms from one another. They're not really hallways but spaces composed of parts of other rooms. Looking through from the porch doors to the kitchen window, for example, you look directly along one pathway, past bookshelves across from the stairway, and then into the kitchen beyond. The window at the far end of this porch-kitchen axis performs a very important function. We are attracted to light and instinctively tend to move toward it. Without this focal window, the draw of the kitchen would be significantly reduced. The passageway between the away room and kitchen is also a usable space—a cross between a library and a stair vestibule.

Openings between rooms are wider than would have been typical in farmhouses of the past, allowing a better view into the adjacent space. The dining area is open to the kitchen, for example, but the room is still defined with a lattice that hints at where the old farmhouse wall would have been. The connection between the living room and the away-room hallway is defined in a similar way. You still have a definite sense of the edge of the room, but the space and view flow out beyond the implied boundary.

At the stairway there's a more substantial lattice—one that looks like a decorative wall from the kitchen side but allows a view through to the kitchen for someone descending the stairs. The lower level of the house is not yet finished, but by leaving

LEFT In a classic farmhouse, there would be only a small door connecting kitchen and dining room, but for today's lifestyle the two rooms need to be much more open to one another. The wide-spaced lattice and columns suggest where the old wall would have been, but the view is wide open.

BELOW To make the most of the farmland vistas, the kitchen work area is wrapped with double-hung windows. The inset cabinets, deep porcelain sink, and maple butcher-block countertops are all reminiscent of an old farmhouse kitchen, while the electrical outlets and period light fixtures have been gracefully integrated to make it work for today's cook.

the stairway open, with a door at the bottom instead of at the top, there's a suggestion of more living space below. And when the lower level is eventually finished, it will feel much more connected to the rest of the house.

A Light-Filled Kitchen

We spend much of our lives in the kitchen today, yet all too often this room is poorly lit and uninspiring. For Susan and David, a light-filled kitchen was high on their list of priorities. One of the pictures they brought to show Jean at their first meeting was a photo of a restored kitchen in a Victorian home, with many windows and wide sills for plants and other kitchen paraphernalia. Jean took this image as the inspiration for their

kitchen. She wrapped the corner with double-hung windows and pulled the kitchen cabinets 4 in. in from the exterior wall to make room for a widened sill. This gives the illusion that the wall is thicker, a reference back to the brick and stone walls of old farmhouses.

What about the lost upper cabinets, which had to be sacrificed to make way for the windows? This kitchen has two substantial pantries: one at the end of the corner countertop and the other across from the island. As long as provisions are made for storage to replace what is lost to windows, a kitchen can function perfectly well. In fact, many people prefer a pantry because the storage space can be laid out more efficiently and made more accessible.

A lowered soffit runs the full length of the kitchen work surface, from the refrigerator at one end to the smaller of the pantries at the other. This soffit, which is the same depth as the countertop below, does a number of things. It creates an alcove, in which the kitchen work happens. It fills out the frame around the windows, giving a greater sense of depth to the wall. And it provides a surface from which to hang the light fixtures, which in this home are period pieces, not the typical recessed cans we've become accustomed to today.

ABOVE With its almost symmetrical gable-end design, corner boards, and simple trim framing double-hung windows, the house looks like it's from an earlier time. The woodwork surrounding the upper vent at the top of the gable is the kind of detail that can make a big impression with only a small amount of effort.

Keeping It Simple

While many Not So Big Houses make a visual statement with bold color schemes, this house succeeds through subtlety. With walls painted a slightly darker color than the bright white trim, the whole house takes on a quiet elegance. The trim itself has a simple profile: The 1x6 baseboards have a piece of cap molding, and the 1x4 trim around the windows and doors has an added backband. These interior details lend the house the proportion and character of its early 20th-century ancestors without creating

RIGHT The wider trim around windows and doors and the shape and size of the baseboards are typical of an older home. It's these seemingly insignificant finish details that give a house much of its character.

an overly careful replica. The same is true of the exterior, with its white clapboard siding, corner boards, and symmetrical windows at the gable ends. The steep 12-in-12 roof and wraparound porch complete the picture.

When we imagine what a farmhouse should be, for most of us it's pretty close to this new home. Our modern tract houses—with their vaulted, textured ceilings, white walls, casement windows, and predictable trimwork—aren't the houses most of us want to come home to. Here we have an example of a house that, through restraint and an appreciation for the past, puts forward a familiar but definitely upgraded vision for the future. It's a farmhouse all right— but a farmhouse for our time.

Architect:
SALA Architects
Builder:
Al Hirsch & Sons
Size: 2,400 sq. ft.
Location:
Chaska, Minn.

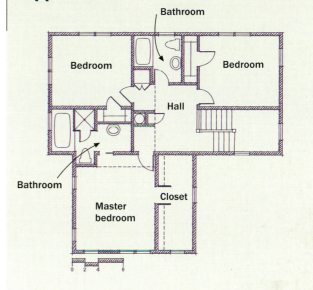

Upper Floor

Perfect Pitch

*B*uilders and architects often refer to the pitch of a roof as a ratio of rise to run, or height to length. You'll hear professionals discussing a house with a "10-in-12 roof" (written as 10:12), which is fairly steep, or a "3-in-12 roof" (written 3:12), which is gently sloped. The first number in the ratio (the rise) is the number of inches the roof rises for every foot of length. The second number (the run) is always 12, for the number of inches in a foot.

Because roof pitch isn't well understood, it's not uncommon for a change to be made in roof slope during design or construction that ruins the look of the house. This farmhouse has a much steeper roof in the two-story sections than in the one-story lean-tos. If the lean-to roofs were built with the same slope as the main house, they would look completely out of proportion, and all resemblance to the farmhouses of the past would be lost.

As you drive around your own neighborhood, notice the difference that roof slope makes to the look and feel of a house. Notice, too, the houses that don't look quite right. Often this is the result of a roof with a slope that doesn't fit the style of the house it shelters.

A Jewel in the Suburbs

ABOVE From the outside, you'd never know what creativity and delight lie within this unassuming little house.

OPPOSITE Removing the wall between the kitchen and dining area helps the two spaces function as one, making the whole house look and live bigger. Color has been used creatively in this area to tie the rooms together visually and continue the playful spirit that characterizes this house. In a small space, a little color goes a long way.

SET IN A SUBURBAN NEIGHBORHOOD of look-alike single-family homes from the 1940s and '50s, Jim and Julie's house is undistinguished from the outside. But step in through the front door, and you're in for a surprise. This house is a veritable jewel box of clever storage and detailing ideas—an extraordinary example of what's possible when you approach design with a playful, inventive spirit and a commitment to doing more with less.

Over the past decade, a miraculous transformation has taken place within the existing walls of this 1,500-sq.-ft. 1950s tri-level. Jim, an interior designer by profession, used his skill to rethink the house and make it a home filled with character, detail, and vitality. Julie used her graphic-design talent to make every surface a composition of color, texture, and light. Both love the unexpected, and both enjoyed the process of letting the house evolve. It took the change well, emerging with the flexible durability needed to accommodate an

This house is an extraordinary example of what's possible when you approach design with a commitment to doing more with less.

Up Close

The television is cleverly concealed in a well-crafted cabinet at the end of the lower kitchen cabinet run. The television faces into the hearth room: As in many homes today, the hearth *is* the television.

active family that includes seven-year-old daughter Racheal and two golden retrievers. Together Jim and Julie have created a home that is both fun to look at and a pleasure to live in.

Opening Up the Rooms

When the couple first moved in, the house had a standard floor plan, with distinct formal and informal spaces. A wall separated the dining room from the kitchen, which was designed, like many homes of the era, as a place solely for food preparation. And, as in most homes today, most of the living took place in the tiny kitchen and breakfast nook, while the formal rooms, which were visually and physically set apart, remained unused. By opening the kitchen and dining room to one another, the house automatically feels bigger because you can see farther, and the entire area becomes the social hub of the house.

Other special touches add to the feeling of spaciousness. In the kitchen, the cabinets are held away from the walls and ceiling to make the room feel bigger. (It would be more typical to make an L-shaped counter at the far corner of the room.) Eliminating cabinets above the peninsula also minimizes the visual separation between the kitchen and dining areas. Jim refers to the peninsula itself as the "runway" between the refrigerator and the chopping block. Thinking about the way food is

Designer:
Garramone Design
Builder:
Jim Garramone
Size: 1,500 sq. ft.
Location:
Evanston, Ill.

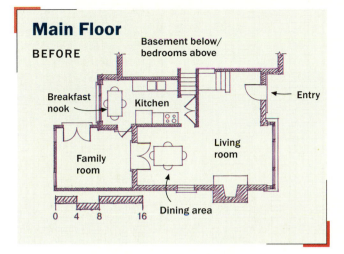

Main Floor

BEFORE

Basement below/bedrooms above

Breakfast nook

Kitchen

Entry

Living room

Family room

Dining area

0   4   8   16

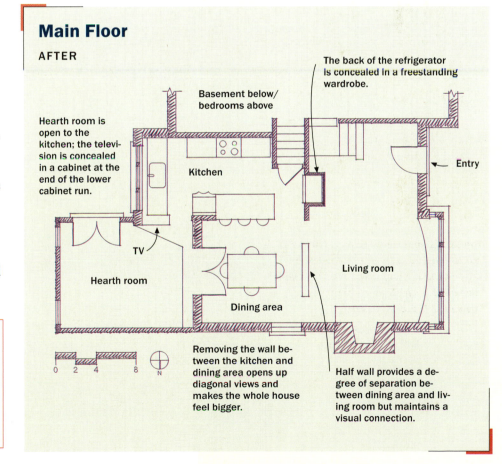

Main Floor

AFTER

The back of the refrigerator is concealed in a freestanding wardrobe.

Basement below/bedrooms above

Hearth room is open to the kitchen; the television is concealed in a cabinet at the end of the lower cabinet run.

Kitchen

Entry

TV

Hearth room

Living room

Dining area

0   2   4   8   N

Removing the wall between the kitchen and dining area opens up diagonal views and makes the whole house feel bigger.

Half wall provides a degree of separation between dining area and living room but maintains a visual connection.

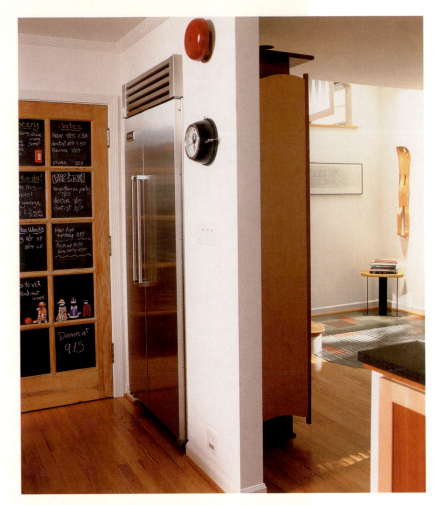

moved through the space is especially important in a small work area.

Making the Most of the Ordinary

The chopping block is a standard end-grain model with added front and back edging detail (see the photo on p. 70). The sculpted front edge is rounded so chopped vegetables can be swept into a bowl held underneath—another example of adding inexpensive and creative detail. The back edging provides a place for knife storage just where you need it—a wonderful example of useful beauty.

Above the chopping block, a standard medicine cabinet—its mirror replaced with cork—serves as both a bulletin board and spice cabinet. Most upper cabinets are 12 in. deep, but that doesn't mean that they all have to be. The shallower cabinet allows for better visual access to the chopping block—always a plus for a work surface. What looks like a

built-in microwave cabinet below the chopping block is, in fact, a clever use of a standard cabinet door. The microwave sits on a shelf, and the surrounding door panel has been cut to fit, with holes above and below to allow for ventilation.

The door to the basement also uses ordinary materials in

ABOVE AND RIGHT The refrigerator installation is a wonderful example of creativity, turning a space-wasting liability into an asset. From the kitchen, it looks like a normal refrigerator. Move into the entryway, and you see a finely crafted free-standing wardrobe—in reality, a camouflage for the back of the refrigerator.

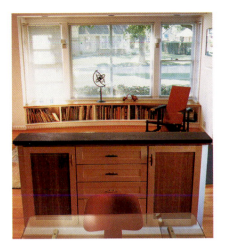

ABOVE This shallow cabinet stores Rachael's drawing and coloring paraphernalia and provides just enough separation between the dining and living areas. The top is soapstone, to match the kitchen countertops. Reusing a particular material around the house lends continuity and integrity.

RIGHT The gentle curve of the bookshelf window seat is an elegant touch that gives the whole room a softness. Introducing curves in nonstructural elements like this adds beauty without excessive cost.

unexpected ways. Jim and Julie replaced the glass in an old French door with a porcelainized steel blackboard, which serves as a message board for the family (see the photo on p. 72). As a bonus, while magnets won't stick to the new stainless-steel refrigerator, they will stick to the steel panels in the French door, allowing it to replace that essential family display area.

Attention to Detail

The careful attention to detail continues in the living room, where the window bay beautifully illustrates the effect a soffit, or lowered ceiling, can have on a room (see the photo on p. 73). If the ceiling height of the rest of the room continued out to the window wall and the bookshelf below were removed, the room would have more volume, but, contrary to what you might expect, it wouldn't feel bigger. If anything, the room would feel smaller. It is the contrast between the two ceiling heights, and the development of two distinct "places," that gives this room its beauty and uniqueness.

LEFT The house has functional works of art at every turn, and this English phone booth is certainly the most unexpected of them. The bedroom level is separated from the main floor by a short flight of stairs, with a landing between the two that used to have a standard railing. Now the phone booth sits there, and one moves through it almost like a gate between the two living areas. Its novelty gives the whole house a sense of whimsy that anticipates more surprises to come.

LEFT On a wall of the hearth room are these narrow shelves, used to display a constantly changing exhibit of photos and drawings.

BELOW There's a comfortable connection between the hearth room and the kitchen, allowing for conversation between the two.

A 36-in.-high storage wall has been located between the dining and living areas, giving some separation between the rooms while still maintaining a visual connection (see the photo on p. 73). The wall allows the living-room furniture to be pushed against it, which effectively increases the floor area available. Without its presence, the chairs would need to be farther away from the dining-room table in order to look right. So by defining the boundary between spaces while maintaining the connecting views, a small space can be made to comfortably accommodate more items.

The Hearth Room

Some further creative remodeling provides a quiet space while opening up yet another vista to the kitchen. The brick wall visible in the photograph used to be the exterior of the house.

BELOW A platform bed doubles as couch, table, and sitting area. The cushions at either end are built around a steel frame for back support. The swivel side tables offer room for a cup of tea and a paperback.

A porch had been added, which Jim and Julie turned into a hearth room that also functions as an away room of sorts. Because the hearth room is separated from the dining area with French doors, one person can watch TV here without disrupting anybody in the living or dining area. When the TV is not in use, it is hidden from view with bifold doors (see the photo on p. 70).

A Not So Big Bedroom

Although the existing bedrooms in the house are not large, Jim and Julie made the most of limited space by designing furniture that serves multiple functions and by keeping broad expanses open to maximize the sense of space. This feeling is further enhanced in the bedroom by the mirrored doors behind the bed, which both serve as a piece of art and double the apparent length of the room. On one wall is a wonderfully clever and beautiful storage area. Rather than building a standard closet, Jim made the available space into both hanging area and dresser, decorating the doors to look like a wall of drawers. The whole composition has become a work of art.

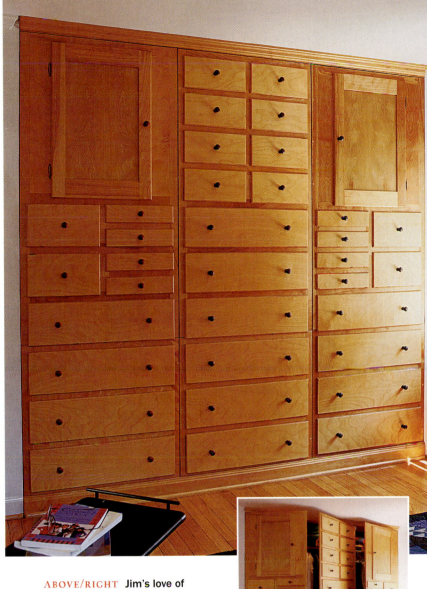

An Illusion of Space

*T*he bathroom off the master bedroom presented a particular challenge, both in the use of space and in access to light. A typical arrangement in a small bathroom like this one is to have a tub with shower rod and curtain that extend across the end of the room, which decreases its apparent size. Here, with a retractable shower rod, the full dimension of the room is apparent.

The selection of fixtures also allows this bathroom to live larger than its diminutive size would suggest. The bath itself is a deep soaking tub. And the pedestal sink opens up more floor space, again increasing the apparent size of the room. As a final touch, the mirror over the sink extends all the way to the ceiling, reflecting the room and adding yet another illusion of space. No opportunity is missed in this house to make an everyday necessity into an inspired composition.

ABOVE/RIGHT **Jim's love of Shaker cabinetry inspired this closet wall. Cleverly designed to look like a wall of drawers, the upper "drawers" are in reality doors that open to reveal a very efficient hanging closet. The lower drawers really are drawers.**

Three
Easy Pieces

Tailoring a house for the way its occupants really live is a fundamental Not So Big concept. When I first started thinking about how to accomplish this, I realized that the best model we have for comfortable, informal living is the weekend cabin. It's designed to be both welcoming and functional and usually includes a strong connection to the outdoors. Rooms are cozy—certainly smaller than we expect in a year-round house—and there are no superfluous spaces. Yet often these weekend retreats make our spirits soar. There's something about their scale and simplicity that gives them a warmth that's missing in a larger home. The idea of nesting, or cocooning, is becoming more and more appealing in our busy lives, but we seem to think we can do it in spacious mansions, when a true nest or cocoon is really a cozy and secure haven, just big enough to accommodate its residents.

It's a rare space that's too small for comfort, but it's not at all uncommon for one to be uncomfortably big.

79

This cabin is a perfect illustration of how it works. Here we have an unembellished version of a house, reduced to its spatial essentials but with the qualities of comfort we're so eager to find. It came about when architect Rick Phillips was asked by his mother and stepfather, Kay and Ted, to design a year-round lake cabin for the family on their island property at the tip of Door County Peninsula in Wisconsin. The site was a five-hour drive and a half-hour boat ride from Rick's home in Chicago, and his frequent weekend visits to the site gave him plenty of time to think about the design.

ABOVE A covered link between the sleeping and living cottages frames the view of the lake beyond, creating a striking vista as you approach the house. (PHOTO COURTESY FREDERICK PHILLIPS.)

Architect:
Frederick Phillips
& Associates

Builder:
Young Brothers
Construction

Size: 1,200 sq. ft.

Location:
Washington Island, Wis.

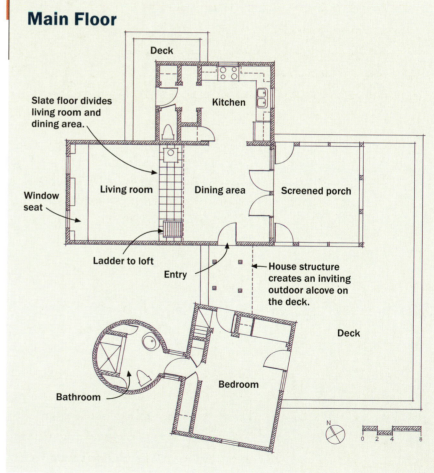

Main Floor

Deck

Kitchen

Slate floor divides living room and dining area.

Living room

Dining area

Screened porch

Window seat

Ladder to loft

Entry

House structure creates an inviting outdoor alcove on the deck.

Deck

Bathroom

Bedroom

N

0 2 4 8

Shelter around Activity

Rick knew that one of the most important spaces for his parents would be the deck, a place to sit and look out at the water. But a deck without a sense of shelter tends to be little used, because it makes you feel vulnerable and exposed. However, if you add some sort of structure to provide a shelter around the various activities, it's suddenly inviting. This can be difficult to do with a traditional rectangular house form. So Rick got creative. His long drive to the property took him past a multitude of farms, with their random collections of agrarian buildings—silos, barns, storage sheds, farmhouses. These images inspired him to consider a similar combination of forms for the cabin. By breaking the structure into three distinct pieces, he could create an outdoor alcove with a sense of containment on three sides.

When Kay and Ted saw the scale model Rick had made to illustrate his concept, they loved the idea. He suggested that each of the three forms contain one of the main functions—living in one, sleeping in another, and bathing in a third—and that they keep the size of each space to a reasonable minimum. Kay and Ted wanted a place that was relatively inexpensive to build and didn't want rooms

ABOVE Sometimes a room is most comfortable when its dimensions are small and it has only a few strategically placed windows, focusing your attention inside rather than out. This living area—with its two symmetrically placed windows, flanking bookshelves, and long window seat—has a distinctly Scandinavian-cottage feel: plain in style but cozy and inviting.

LEFT The kitchen, which is an alcove off the main rectangle of living space, contains just the bare necessities, with open shelves instead of upper cabinets. The lower cabinets and flooring are made of natural cedar, which gives this simple room a deep richness.

No matter how large or small a house, the need for different levels of privacy is a critical design element.

that seemed designed more for large gatherings than for family living. To them, the cabin was a place of retreat from the hubbub of city life, and they weren't interested in having a lot of space to maintain.

Fear of "Too Smallness"

In the final design, the living room is only 14 ft. wide, which most people would consider too narrow. But at this dimension, the couch and chairs can be nestled against opposite walls of the room and still be a comfortable distance apart for conversation. The window seat that runs the length of the far end of the room completes the sitting circle and provides space for an additional guest or two.

All too often, we increase the size of a room in the planning phase, for fear it will feel too small. But making this room even 2 ft. wider would dramatically reduce its intimacy. It's this fear of "too smallness" that is driving our houses to reach proportions more appropriate to giants than humans. And in the process, we're losing the very quality that makes us feel at home.

The Shape of the Ceiling

The main level is straightforward in plan: just a long rectangle with a kitchen alcove opening off to the north side. From the plan, you might imagine that the living and dining areas would look very similar, since they're almost identical in shape. But the ceiling heights and forms are quite different, giving the spaces a very different feel. In the living area, the ceiling is gently sloped,

Up Close

A low wainscot runs around all the living spaces in the house, creating the effect of a waterline around the main level. The darker coloring of everything below this line emphasizes the lower section of each space, adding a visual weight that subtly encourages you to sit down and stay a while.

TOP AND ABOVE The bathrooms on both levels are enclosed in the windowless silo, giving each a cocoon-like feel. The rooms aren't dark, though. They get ample light from the short, window-filled walkway (visible in the exterior photo) that connects them to the bedrooms.

following the lean-to form of the roof above, with a view to the upper-level loft. By contrast, the dining area is sheltered below the loft and has a flat 8-ft.-high ceiling that's paneled with wood, giving it added visual weight.

The difference between the two spaces is further accentuated by the wall of French doors at the far end of the dining area, which open onto the porch beyond. This is the source of most of the light and views and so tends to lead one outward, while the living area is inward looking and encourages nesting. What looks almost boring and undifferentiated in plan is far from it when seen in all three dimensions.

Public and Private

In any cabin, there's often a lot of shared time, but there's also a need for varying degrees of privacy. Despite its small size, this cabin offers a full spectrum of spaces. There are those that are clearly very public, such as the living and dining areas. Then there's the loft, a semiprivate space where the activities below can be heard but not seen—useful when you want a private space without feeling isolated from the rest of the family. And finally, there's the complete privacy offered by a separate structure for sleeping, where noise from the living cabin can't even be heard.

No matter how large or small a house, the need for different levels of privacy is a critical design element. A home can look very beautiful but actually be quite unlivable because there's no place to be alone. Or it can go to the opposite extreme, with every space so separate that there's no sense of focus, no central gathering place. This cabin gets the balance just right. If you want a house to work well, it's important to place the main living areas where they can be seen easily from several other places. The main spaces gain much of their vitality from their visibility.

The private spaces should be tucked away, off the beaten track, where someone seeking privacy can draw back from the social center and know that they'll be left alone. The places in the middle of the public/private spectrum, like the loft in this house, can be designed to participate in some of the energy of the focal gathering places but give the occupants the option to engage in the activities or not, as they choose.

Even when a house is very small, there's no reason it can't offer a spatial and social variety of places for living. When we design each space to enhance the activity it houses, rather than worrying about whether it is big enough for the rare occasions when we have extra guests, our houses benefit enormously.

We can learn a lot from a weekend cabin like this one. What we seek in our year-round homes is some of the ease and informality we see here. This comes from building only what you need, tailoring it to fit your *real* lifestyle, and crafting it to bring delight to the senses. It sounds easy, but there are a lot of countervailing forces at work to convince us otherwise. Just keep in mind that it's a rare space that's too small for comfort, but it's not at all uncommon for one to be uncomfortably big.

ABOVE The covered link provides protection and enclosure for the deck. If you imagine these two structures without the connecting roof, the space looks more like a hallway than a sheltered place.

LEFT There's something fascinating about a round window. When placed at the center of a gable, as in this loft, it symbolizes both focus and inspiration. The effect is dramatic and worth the added expense.

A Sense of Flow

ABOVE AND RIGHT By enclosing the existing carports and extending a colonnade beyond the face of the house, the architect completely altered the sense of entry. (PHOTO AT RIGHT COURTESY BERNIE BAKER.)

WHEN IT COMES TO HOUSING needs, empty nesters are faced with a real dilemma. The house that served so well while the children were growing up no longer works so well for two. Yet they want to stay put because they've developed close relationships in the community over the years. This is where their friends live. This is the place they love. Fortunately, there is an answer: Take your existing house, one designed for the way you lived half a lifetime ago, and transform it into the house of your dreams—a house that fits the way you live today.

This is what Sally and Gary did. Until they met architect Bernie Baker, they were starting to despair of ever getting the house they wanted. They'd been trying to find an architect who understood their desire to completely transform their home, and they knew that applying cosmetic solutions to problem areas wasn't going to be enough. Although a major remodel would be expensive, they loved their wooded canyon site and had no de-

This house uses the principles of building Not So Big to make an adequate house into a really comfortable home, tailored to the lives of the people who live there.

OPPOSITE The colonnade continues on the inside of the house, serving as a spine that defines the circulation space and organizes both rooms and views. New windows extend all the way to the roof, minimizing the distinction between inside and out.

ABOVE The brick courtyard between the two garages serves as a light-filled ante-room to the house. Standing here, you are welcomed by the house before ever stepping across the threshold.

sire to leave. Bernie was the first architect they'd met who understood. He told them that what their house needed was a sense of flow, both of movement and of views, something sorely missing prior to the remodel.

Redefining the Entry

In the original structure, an unassuming split entry, you were greeted at every turn by obstructing walls, dark hallways, and visual cues that misled. As you walked into the old house, for example, the view led your eye directly to the master bedroom. Visitors to the house felt drawn to a room that was part of the private realm—not a direction they were welcome to proceed in. Meanwhile, the lower level, where the main living areas were located, was shrouded in darkness.

Bernie recognized the need to redefine the process of entering the house, to give the appropriate cues as to which way to proceed and to make the descent into the main body of the house a pleasant and inviting experience. Just like a choreographer, he composed a remodeling with a new theme and variations, superimposed on the bones of the old house. The result is a home that, though not a lot bigger, has integrity and style. It uses the principles of building Not So Big to make an adequate house into a really comfortable home, tailored to the lives of the people who live there.

Entering is an extraordinarily important part of experiencing a house. If you're not welcomed by the house as you enter, it's difficult to remedy the negative impression once you're inside. So Bernie started back at the driveway with design strategies that would help to establish a sequence of places to draw you into the house. He enclosed the two carports on either side of the entry walk, added a skylight above the doorway, and included lots of glass in and around the front door. The result is both welcoming and inviting.

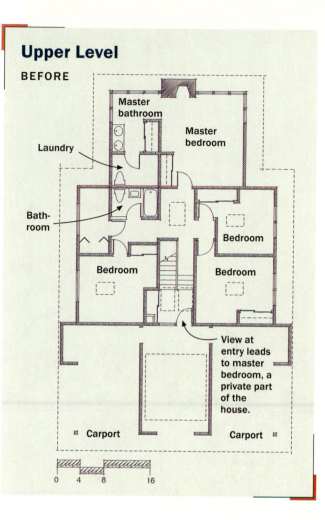

Upper Level

BEFORE

Master bathroom

Master bedroom

Laundry

Bath-room

Bedroom

Bedroom

Bedroom

View at entry leads to master bedroom, a private part of the house.

Carport   Carport

0   4   8   16

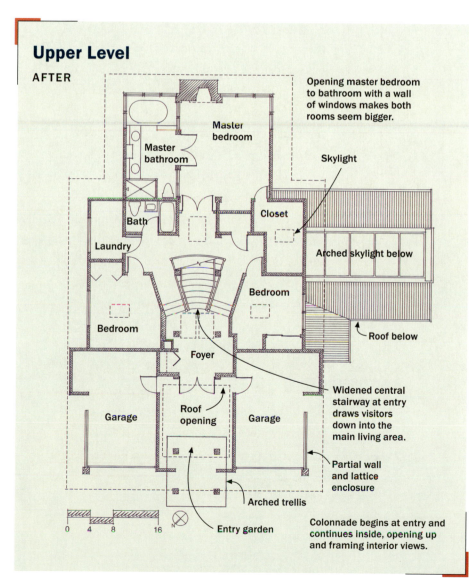

Upper Level

AFTER

Opening master bedroom to bathroom with a wall of windows makes both rooms seem bigger.

Master bedroom

Master bathroom

Skylight

Bath

Closet

Laundry

Arched skylight below

Bedroom

Roof below

Bedroom

Foyer

Widened central stairway at entry draws visitors down into the main living area.

Garage

Roof opening

Garage

Partial wall and lattice enclosure

Arched trellis

0   4   8   16   N

Entry garden

Colonnade begins at entry and continues inside, opening up and framing interior views.

Entering is an extraordinarily important part of experiencing a house. If you're not welcomed by the house as you enter, it's difficult to remedy the negative impression once you're inside.

Interior Views

Bernie established a colonnade that extends just beyond the face of the house, defining the entry and welcoming guests with its trellised arch. The colonnade continues inside and runs through the entire house, giving order and coherence to the existing structure. It becomes a device for opening up and framing interior views and serves to orient movement through the house: Where the eye is led, the feet will follow. By relocating the up-stairways to either side of the down-stairway, the inviting path lies directly ahead. As you stand at the doorway, your gaze is directed down through the gradually widening stairs to the living-room fireplace beyond. Although you can still see the master-bedroom fireplace, it's clear from the location of the railing that you're *not* invited to proceed this way.

The colonnade runs through the entire house, giving order and coherence to the existing structure.

ABOVE In the old house, the front entry gave mixed messages about which way to go. Now, the widened and centered down-stairway clearly indicates that this is the way to proceed. Although the distance up to the master bedroom suite is shorter, the railing sends a clear but subtle signal that this view is just for looking.

RIGHT The colonnade continues down to the lower level, where the final two columns flank the fireplace. Having such a focal point to walk toward helps draw people into the heart of the house.

Designing for the Way You Live

Once you are down the first flight of stairs, you're met with a surprise—another level of living space quite invisible from the entry foyer. Here, significant changes have been made to reconfigure this space to work with the way Sally and Gary really live. Instead of an enclosed kitchen that's dark, uninspiring, and isolated from the main living spaces, the kitchen opens to an informal sitting area, where Gary (who is not the cook in this household) can sit and talk to Sally while she prepares dinner.

Sally and Gary both love to entertain, and the only added space in this remodeling project is a formal dining room—a spectacular room that is delightful to look at, even when it's not in use (see the photo on p. 92). For people who seldom entertain or who like to entertain only informally, a dining room is a largely superfluous space today. But for people like Sally and Gary, who really enjoy putting on a spread in a room with a special ambiance, the dining room is one of the most important rooms in the house. The Not So Big philosophy doesn't dictate that you get rid of all formal spaces. If you actually use a formal dining room for formal dining (and not just as a place to drop off the mail), by all means include one. The point is to design for the way *you* live.

Sally prepares dinner for friends and family several times a month, and this new dining space provides the perfect stage for her culinary productions. A 20-ft.-long skylight stretches across the new space and extends into the kitchen, making a once-dark

TOP The remodeled kitchen has been opened up and made into the nerve center of the house. A sitting space adjacent to the kitchen allows Gary to chat with Sally as she prepares dinner.

ABOVE A television is cleverly concealed in the back side of the kitchen cabinetry. When the doors are closed, there's no sign it's there at all.

Lower Level
BEFORE

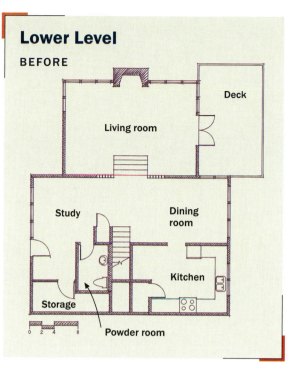

Deck

Living room

Study

Dining room

Kitchen

Storage

Powder room

0 2 4 8

Lower Level
AFTER

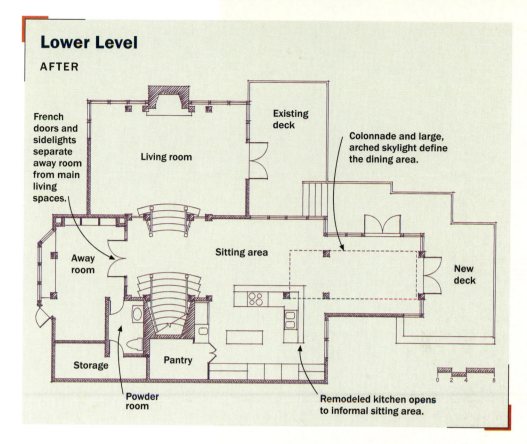

French doors and sidelights separate away room from main living spaces.

Existing deck

Colonnade and large, arched skylight define the dining area.

Living room

Away room

Sitting area

New deck

Storage

Pantry

Powder room

Remodeled kitchen opens to informal sitting area.

0 2 4 8

and inhospitable area into a room filled with light and warmth. In a sunnier climate, such a large skylight might cause serious overheating, but in the Pacific Northwest, such concerns are minimal. With so many cloudy days, finding ways to introduce natural light becomes the governing issue.

The kitchen itself is like the helm of a ship—a place from which all others can be seen—and very much in keeping with the style of the rest of the house. A wide, beamlike soffit lowers the ceiling height around the kitchen, defining the room without the use of walls. Here, Sally keeps her collection of pottery and china in glass cabinets surrounding the double ovens. With internal lighting, they become a beautiful backdrop to the main work area. When it's just the two of them, Sally and Gary will often eat at the small table in the middle of the kitchen, which also doubles as a kitchen island. Substituting a table for a built-in island can lend a farmhouse informality to a room, making it seem homey and approachable.

Architect:
Bernie Baker
Architect, P.S.
Size: 2,600 sq. ft.
Location:
Mercer Island, Wash.

RIGHT A raised countertop shields kitchen work areas from view without the need for enclosing walls. The lowered soffit further defines the room and provides a place from which to hang pendant lights.

OPPOSITE For many families, a dining room is superfluous. Not so for this couple, who entertain in this garden-room setting two or three times a month. The room is so enchanting that guests will linger long after the meal is over.

ABOVE Although the windows in this house—custom made by a local craftsman—were clearly an expensive item, they have an enormous impact. There's light at every turn, and the composition of shapes and sizes becomes a work of art. The pattern created by the lower and upper windows gives the whole house an underlying rhythm.

BELOW A wall was removed between the master bedroom and the adjoining bathroom and replaced by a bank of storefront windows. This new configuration allows visual access to the light and beauty of the bathroom from the bedroom and also makes the entire suite feel significantly larger.

Storefront Windows

Another space that hadn't worked well in the original house was the study, which was too open to the rest of the house for concentrated work. By separating this area from the main living spaces with French doors and flanking sidelights—what Bernie refers to as "storefront windows"—the room has become an ideal away room. Sally uses this space for her business (writing children's books) and when the television is on in the sitting area beside the kitchen, the study can become a quiet retreat without losing its visual connection to the social hub of the house.

The master bedroom also uses a wall of windows to make both bedroom and bathroom feel bigger and to flood the bedroom with light. Bathrooms are often beautiful rooms, with built-in cabinetry and broad expanses of mirror. Opening this view to the master bedroom gives a gracious and airy feel without adding any square footage. This same trick is used throughout the house, where almost every sight line, whether to another interior space or out to the trees beyond, is captured or framed by a wall of glass. The effect is much more dramatic than settling for one or two windows set into a wall surface, as is the norm in most new construction.

Clearly, this was not an inexpensive remodel. It would have cost only slightly more to build new. But for a couple whose goal was to take what they already had and transform it, this remodeling responds masterfully—not by adding

The Away Room

One of the biggest problems in today's homes is the pervasive presence of noisy entertainment like television and computer games. When the TV is on in a room, it tends to capture everyone's attention—even those who would rather be doing something else. As we build more open floor plans, the problem gets worse. What we need is a space in the home that allows the activities that require peace and quiet to be separated from those that generate noise.

One solution, and a common feature of a Not So Big House, is an away room. This is a compact, multipurpose space, usually about the size of a small bedroom, that opens onto the main living area with French doors. Its primary role is to provide an acoustically private activity space that's still visually connected to the living area and kitchen. It can also serve as a study during the day and can even convert to a guest bedroom for visitors. In this home, Sally's study is an excellent example of an away room. The wide French doors and surrounding windows offer ample connecting views to the living area and kitchen, so she doesn't feel isolated. But with the doors closed, the TV can be on and Sally can still get her work done.

The away room is also wonderfully effective when there are children in the house. With the television and electronic toys confined in this room, children can enjoy themselves to their exuberant hearts' content, and the sounds of Nintendo won't prevent adult conversation. The glass doors allow parents and children to see one another, which is great for supervising, and also provides kids with a comfortable sense of family togetherness.

more square footage but by revising what was already there to meet the needs of today. Even the plainest of houses often has good bones that, with the vision of an architect, can have new life breathed into it. Why throw away what you don't want anymore just because your lifestyle has changed? Instead, why not tailor it to fit who you are today?

A House in Harmony

THERE'S GROWING CONCERN IN OLDER suburbs today about a building phenomenon known as "tear-downs." This happens when a house in an established and desirable neighborhood is purchased, torn down, and replaced with a new house. The sad reality is that the new house is frequently a massive and ostentatious structure, similar to the starter castles so prevalent in newer housing developments across the country. Such a house is of a completely different scale and character than its older neighbors, and it often offends the residents of the existing community.

This is rarely done intentionally. The buyers of the older house select it because they like the neighborhood. But when it comes to remodeling versus starting from scratch, there's no contest. A new house will invariably end up costing less than renovating the old one and will provide more of the amenities we expect in a home. So the new owners select a house from a plan book, with no consideration of how the house will relate to the neighborhood.

This house makes more with less at every turn, using restraint to create a composition with depth and beauty.

OPPOSITE The fireplace in the family room is a marvelous composition of fireslate and wood that plays off the proportions of both the house and the Golden Mean. Although nothing is quite symmetrical, everything is beautifully balanced to appeal to the eye. If you look closely, you'll see that even the slate on the floor has been cut to line up with the edges of the materials on the wall.

A Not So Big House is a good neighbor, custom-made to fit the needs of its owners and also to fit into its surroundings.

ABOVE Colors and textures were carefully selected to give the house a subtle distinctiveness. Because the lines of the windows are so fine, their bright red coloring is not overbearing but, like well-applied makeup, draws the eye back for a second look. In texture, the plywood panels of the upper story contrast with the narrow lap siding of the area below. But because they are both stained the same color, the effect is one of restraint.

Good Neighbors

It was just such a situation that Amy and Frank faced when they purchased a house for themselves and their two small children in an upscale Lexington neighborhood of 1960s split levels. Although they had originally planned to add on, they quickly discovered that it would be far less expensive to start from scratch with a new home. But they were also concerned about their neighbors and wanted to help maintain the character of the community they'd just joined.

Fortunately, they found an alternative to the teardown syndrome. Their architect, Paul Lukez, designed a house for them that is a wonderful example of what is so special about building Not So Big. A Not So Big House is a good neighbor, custom-made to fit the needs of its owners and also to fit into its surroundings, adding both beauty and vitality to the community. Paul assured Amy and Frank that the house they wanted, though slightly larger than most of its neighbors, could be made to fit in gracefully. He accomplished this by including the neighborhood's character as one of the site considerations that are a normal part of the architectural process.

Making the new house an exact replica of neighboring homes was not the goal. But by duplicating certain stylistic traits, such as roof slope, window alignments, and the scale of the house facade, the new home would seem a natural and integrated part of the existing fabric of the community. And this indeed is what resulted. The exterior has an understated confidence that lets it blend in with its neighbors while still maintaining its own distinctive character.

Music to Live By

The longer you look at this house, the more there is to see, both inside and out. This is largely because the house has been carefully and beautifully composed. Because the budget was relatively tight, the plan was kept very simple, the rooms straightforward in form, the ceilings flat in most places, and the palette of materials limited. Money was spent instead on making the most of the combinations of materials and the interplay among them.

Gracefully integrating a stairway's handrails is always a challenge. Here, the architect has used a wood that contrasts with the cherry railing and has separated the two rails at the landing. They're almost like arms reaching around the wall and drawing the composition together—a lot more elegant than the standard solution.

LEFT Throughout this home there's an intriguing interplay of dimension and proportion. The side light next to the front door is adjacent to a copper-covered panel with the same dimensions. The two combined exactly match the width of the door.

Main Floor

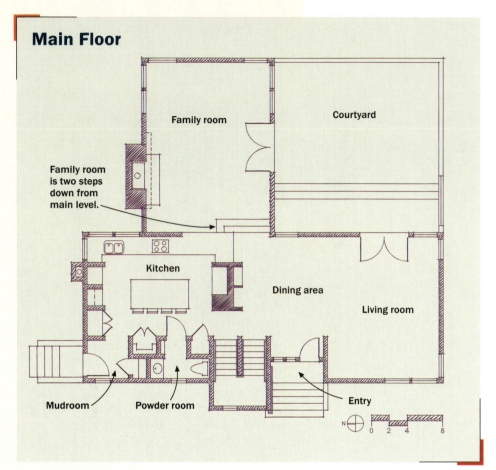

Family room

Courtyard

Family room is two steps down from main level.

Kitchen

Dining area

Living room

Mudroom

Powder room

Entry

N 0 2 4 8

Architect:
Paul Lukez
Architecture

Builder:
Merrill Nearis,
MBN Construction

Size: 3,000 sq. ft.

Location:
Lexington, Mass.

RIGHT Although nothing on the outside of the house seems to align precisely with the elements above or below, there's an underlying order here that makes it look "right." Trace a line down from the edge of each window on the second floor, and you'll see that it lines up with a center divider of either a door or a copper panel below.

It was Goethe who said that architecture is frozen music, and just like a fine piece of music, this house has rhythms and patterns that ripple through the work. Look at the way the materials are used on the exterior. Instead of every surface receiving the same treatment, there are variations in texture, ranging from exterior-grade plywood to lap siding to copper panels, all subtly interlaced with trim bands of a slightly lighter color. In addition to this creative use of materials, there is a proportional relationship among the parts of the house that helps give it its lyrical quality.

Paul likes to set up an architectural language of elements for each house he designs, based on a repetition of connections, materials, and geometric proportions—much like the tempo and key signature of a musical composition. The motif for this house includes an 8-ft. module that can be subdivided into 4-ft., 16-in., and 4-in. dimensions as appropriate. The windows and their surrounding trim, for example, are 4 ft. wide and, when doubled for two windows, 8 ft. wide. Each window contains a pattern of mullions that are based on a 4-in. module. Though they vary slightly from window to window, there's an obvious similarity among them. To borrow a musical term, you can think of this subtle repetition of elements as a theme and variations.

Proportion and Geometry

These relationships don't stop at the windows; the same dimensions are repeated in all the major design features of the house. Both the backsplash behind the cooktop and the fireplace in the family room are dramatic and playful variations on the modular theme. As Paul puts it, "The rules I set for myself provide the constraints for the composition, but the poetry comes from breaking a rule or two. It's a bit like jazz that way." And the backsplash and fireplace are definitely the soloists.

Both of these features comply with most, though not all, of Paul's own constraints, but in addition they engage a propor-

RIGHT The family room is two steps down from the rest of the main level, giving it a higher ceiling and a sense of definition much like that of a quiet pool at the end of a stream. The fireplace and its surrounding woodwork give the room a sense of movement, accentuated by the pencil-line U-channels set between sheets of drywall.

BELOW Natural light was an important design element in this house, with windows situated for maximum effect throughout the day. There are occasional surprises, too, like this window that seems to break through the ceiling to allow in light from above, washing the wall with afternoon sunshine.

tioning system known as the Golden Mean, which appeals to the eye like a harmonious chord does to the ear. In fact, if you study the history of architecture, you'll discover that many of the best-loved buildings have been developed around the proportions of the Golden Mean. Paul doesn't always try to lay out those proportions when he's designing, but intuitively they seem to arise.

This house makes more with less at every turn, using restraint to create a composition with depth and beauty. Its modular theme allows materials to be conserved, at the same time providing the impetus for the creativity that is woven throughout the house. With the kind of discipline that Paul uses to evolve his designs, every material plays its part in making architectural harmony. And it does so while staying in tune with its community. It's a neighbor that all of us could live with.

Phi and the Golden Mean

A proportion is a relationship between lengths that always stays constant, no matter the size. So, for example, a rectangle with the proportion 1:2 ("one to two") retains that proportion whether it is 10 ft. by 20 ft. or 2 in. by 4 in. The proportion called the Golden Mean is 1:1.618. It is also known as phi, the 21st letter of the Greek alphabet.

Like its better-known relative pi, phi has some truly astonishing characteristics. For example, the length of each bone in each finger of our hands has the ratio of phi with respect to the adjoining bone. Its proportions are present throughout all living things, from the distribution of leaves around a stem to the pattern of seeds in a sunflower to the spiral of divisions in a nautilus shell. Phi also underlies the structure and geometry of much in our world that strikes us as beautiful. It's like a hidden harmonic scale—one we have no words for but which many of us can see and feel, even if we have no training in the visual arts. It's the spatial equivalent of having an ear for music.

The house shown here is finely tuned to the Golden Mean. In the drawing below, you'll see the phi proportion occurring over and over, as it spirals down from the plane of the wall to the smallest details on the fireplace. Though we don't yet have the language to describe the harmonics of the Golden Mean, many Not So Big Houses are pleasing not only because of their crafting but also because they are tuned to this hidden scale.

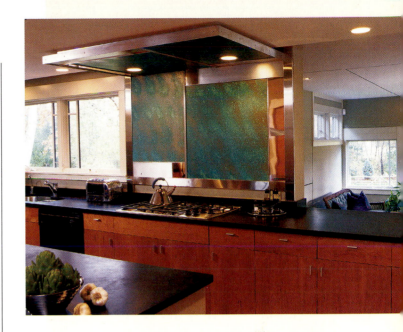

ABOVE There can't be many people who have given as much care and attention to their kitchen backsplash as this family. Designed by the architect as a play on the geometrical proportioning that underlies the whole house, the copper panels are the same dimensions as the adjacent windows. The right-hand panel is full size, while the one on the left is the size of the window minus its left-hand pane.

The backsplash behind the cooktop and the fireplace in the family room are dramatic and playful variations on the modular theme.

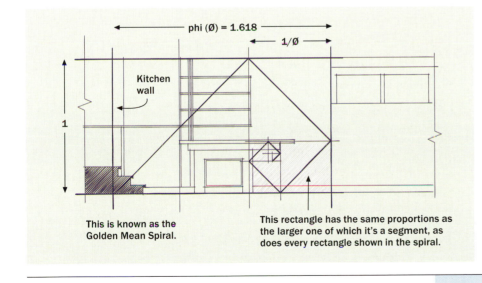

phi (Ø) = 1.618

1/Ø

1

Kitchen wall

This is known as the Golden Mean Spiral.

This rectangle has the same proportions as the larger one of which it's a segment, as does every rectangle shown in the spiral.

Affordable Comfort

ABOVE Although the form of this house is simple, the dark green trim, corner boards, and columns highlight its shape and bring out its personality. The diamond motif above the dormer window adds a playful touch that distinguishes it from a standard builder home at very little expense.

THIS HOUSE, DESIGNED BY ARCHITECT Ross Chapin for a family of four in Amherst, Massachusetts, presents another view of the archetypal qualities that speak to us of home. Like the house in Pennsylvania designed by Jeremiah Eck (see p. 40), it has a steep roof with living space below, a magnificent brick chimney, a front dormer with a focal window, and a central front door under its own sheltering roof. This home, however, was constructed on a much tighter budget, proving that you can build a truly beautiful home even if there isn't a lot of money available. You simply have to evaluate what's important to you and distribute the money accordingly.

When a house is small, it's important to have at least one area that gives a sense of spaciousness.

For Rene and Susan and their two teenage children, the location of the house was a high priority, and like many people, they

OPPOSITE The brick chimney is a dramatic feature that the owners decided to spend extra money on. The layout of the bricks in the chimney recalls the diamond motif from the front of the house. A belt line divides the gable end, separating the cedar shingles above from the lap siding below. The total composition looks both cozy and inviting. (PHOTO BY CHARLES MILLER; COURTESY *FINE HOMEBUILDING* MAGAZINE.)

ended up spending more of their overall budget on land than they had intended. So when it came time for the design process, they knew they'd have to make some compromises. Ross helped them identify what spaces they really needed and explained how to design them to get the most value for their money.

Common Ground

Rene and Susan's previous home had a formal living room, a dining room, and a tiny kitchen on the main level. As in many households, even though there was no family room, the living room still didn't get used much. Instead, the living happened mostly in the kitchen and adjacent dining room. So in their new home, Ross suggested making one large common room, with a

ABOVE A wood stove at the center of the common room shares the chimney with the exterior fireplace. The detailing on the surrounding brickwork gives it the look of a real fireplace, but the wood stove offers a more controllable and efficient heat source. The door to the right of the hearth leads to the deck, which is an extension of the primary living space. (PHOTO BY CHARLES MILLER; COURTESY *FINE HOMEBUILDING* MAGAZINE.)

Architect:
Ross Chapin Architects

Builder:
Bill O'Bremski

Size: 1,750 sq. ft.

Location:
Amherst, Mass.

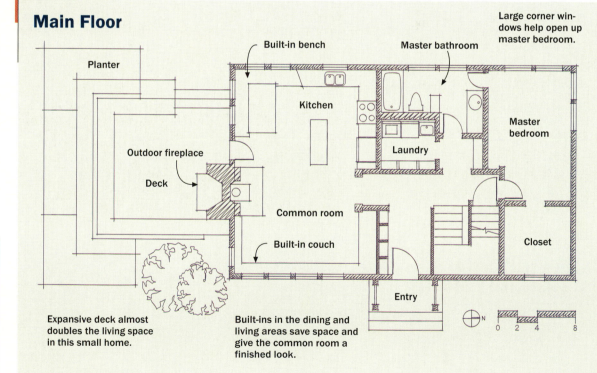

Main Floor

Large corner windows help open up master bedroom.

Built-in bench

Master bathroom

Planter

Kitchen

Master bathroom

Master bedroom

Outdoor fireplace

Laundry

Deck

Common room

Closet

Built-in couch

Entry

N
0 2 4 8

Expansive deck almost doubles the living space in this small home.

Built-ins in the dining and living areas save space and give the common room a finished look.

Built-in furniture can save a significant amount of square footage and give the room a cozy feel at the same time.

high ceiling and lots of light, where the family could congregate to cook, eat, do homework, and socialize. It would be beautiful and filled with warm materials that encouraged both family and friends to linger.

When a house is small, it's important to have at least one area that gives a sense of spaciousness, and in this house the common room serves that function. At 16 ft. by 24 ft. with a 10-ft. ceiling, it's still not a large space for what is essentially three living areas: kitchen, dining room, and living room. But combining them into a single large space creates the illusion of being in a bigger house while using far less square footage than building a separate room for each function.

ABOVE Windows surround the built-in couches in the living room, flooding the space with light and views during the day. By night, the lighting is very simple but effective, with inexpensive wall sconces pointed both up, to bounce light off the ceiling, and down, to create warm pools of light for reading.

Built-In Benefits

Another interesting spatial trick helps the common room stretch even farther. An everyday dining table typically requires at least 3 ft. to 4 ft. between the table edge and the wall, so that there's

ABOVE The kitchen occupies one corner of the rectangle of the main room. To the right, the lowered soffit helps to give the space a sense of shelter and its own identity. To the left, a **built-in bench** on two sides of the table allows the eating area to occupy less space than usual because there's no need to allow for chair clearances on these sides.

room for chairs and some additional circulation space. Here, the chairs are replaced with a built-in bench, so there's no need to allow for that extra space. Built-in furniture can save a significant amount of square footage and give the room a cozy feel at the same time.

The same space-saving design is used in the living area, where the couch is built in along the window wall (see the photo on p. 107). Pushing standard furniture tight against a wall tends to suggest that a room is too small, as if the furniture had to be shoe-horned in. Built-in furniture lets you use a reduced amount of space but gives the opposite effect, making a room look more finished. The continuous lines of the built-in couch, together with the wide windowsill that serves as a shelf, give this room a tailored look and provide ample seating in a modest amount of space.

When you build in couches and benches like this, it's critical that they fit the people who sit in them. Not all chair shapes are comfortable for all people, so Ross arranged for a mockup to be made prior to final construction to make sure that the proportions were just right. Although this is a little extra work and expense, it's money and effort well spent. Remember, you're tailoring a house that is designed to fit *you*.

The Warmth of Wood

The common room also has some finishing details that you wouldn't normally find in an inexpensive home. The cherry cabinetry, made by a local cabinetmaker, is of exceptional quality and beauty. Spending a little extra on the cabinetry can lend the whole house an aura of quality and craftsmanship.

LEFT Kitchen cabinets can be designed to suit your individual needs and to create a custom look. This cabinetry includes an island that's more like a freestanding table. Narrow drawers below the upper cabinets and open shelving in the hard-to-reach areas above the refrigerator and range hood give this inventive kitchen a well-proportioned and hospitable feel.

Up Close

Granite is a beautiful and durable material for countertops and backsplashes, but its cost can be prohibitive. An alternative is to use 12-in. by 12-in. granite tiles, which have the feel and durability of solid granite at a fraction of the cost.

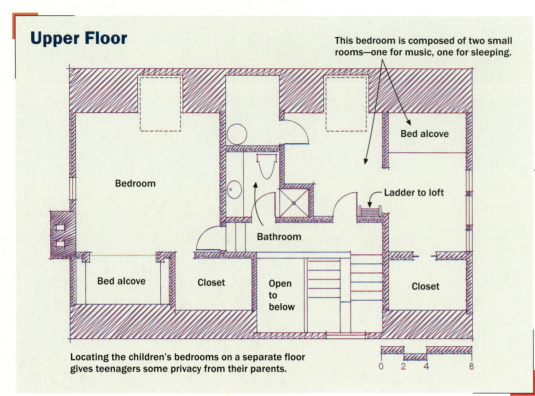

Upper Floor

This bedroom is composed of two small rooms—one for music, one for sleeping.

Bedroom

Bed alcove

Bed alcove

Closet

Bathroom

Ladder to loft

Open to below

Closet

0 2 4 8

Locating the children's bedrooms on a separate floor gives teenagers some privacy from their parents.

The ceiling is another place where a little extra detailing has been added to great effect. Ross had been studying traditional Japanese architecture and was inspired in the creation of this design by the ceiling support system of beams and purlins in the famous temple at Ise. Its open structure allows light to play over the tops of the beams, giving the whole ceiling a floating, latticed quality.

The beams and purlins (the crosspieces) provide the support for the upper level and are made of construction-grade wood, complete with knots and other blemishes. This provided an opportunity to use a lower grade of trim around the windows and doors, to echo that look and save money at the same time. It's very different from the refinement of the cabinetry, yet it works well in this eclectic space.

The trimwork in a house can be a significant expense, so if you can make a less expensive product work for you, it can add up to substantial savings. It's a common fear that choosing a lower grade for one material will ruin the whole effect of the house, but this is seldom the case. By spending more of your budget on highly visible features like the cabinetry and doing some creative compromising elsewhere, the quality of the whole house increases.

By spending more of your budget on highly visible features like the cabinetry and doing some creative compromising elsewhere, the quality of the whole house increases.

Comfort Zones

Beyond the common room, the house is basically unadorned and the spaces are small. But Ross used some interesting design concepts to help make a little go a long way. He separated the private areas of the house into different zones—a children's zone and an adults' zone. This strategy gives family members some privacy from one another, a desirable feature for everyone during the teen years. The second floor of the house is given over to the children, and the adults have their private territory in the main-floor master bedroom. This room isn't intended for socializing, so it was kept intentionally small, with no separate sitting area or extra floor space.

The children's rooms are somewhat larger, to give each child his or her own private realm, well away from mom and dad. Placing the beds in alcoves in the eaves leaves more usable space for everyday activities. Suzanne has a bedroom with lots of floor space, while Stephen's room is actually two small rooms with a wide doorway in between. An aspiring musician, he practices his guitar in one room and uses the other for sleeping. Since both kids' bedrooms are built into the roof form, they have sloped ceilings, which adds some personality without additional expense.

LEFT In a Not So Big House, it's important to make the most of the space that's available. This house employs a number of clever storage ideas, like these staircase bookshelves. Adding 10 in. to the width of the stairway created over 16 lineal feet of book storage, where typically there's just a wall.

BELOW The sloped ceiling of the second floor, which is tucked snugly into the roof form, makes a wonderful, tentlike place for a child's bedroom. A skylight introduces the same amount of light as an expensive dormer, at a fraction of the cost. (PHOTO BY CHARLES MILLER; COURTESY *FINE HOMEBUILDING* MAGAZINE.)

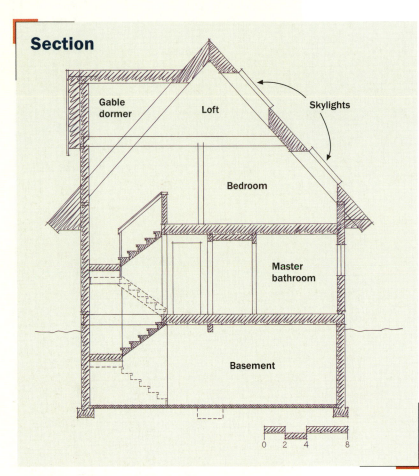

Section

Gable dormer

Loft

Skylights

Bedroom

Master bathroom

Basement

0 2 4 8

Room at the Top

Making full use of all the available space, there's one more room at the top of the house—a loft that's accessed by a ship's ladder. The space is tiny and only 7 ft. high at the ridge, but its diminutive size doesn't mean it's not frequently used. Since the home was built a decade ago, the loft has served as both in-home office and retreat space—a place to go to meditate or simply to sit quietly and be alone. Although this function is not commonly accommodated in most American homes, its inclusion can make an enormous difference in the feeling of spaciousness. You don't need large rooms to make space for privacy. Just the knowledge that there's a getaway at the top of the stairs is all it takes.

It's thoughtful touches like these that give this simple house such a feeling of home. Standing outside, you know instinctively that you'll feel comfortable the moment you step inside.

It's not a pretentious house. It's not designed to impress the neighbors. Instead, it's built to nurture and delight the people who really count—the people who live in it. It has the genuineness that comes from designing for real people and real lives, lived within the confines of a real budget. Most of us know those constraints but don't know how to transcend them. This house admirably shows how it can be done.

RIGHT A small loft accessed by a ship's ladder is a place for individual family members to be alone. Providing a retreat place can make a small house seem larger, because there is room to get away.

OPPOSITE A beautifully designed exterior fireplace extends the season for outdoor socializing and is a great attraction for friends and family alike. With its encircling wooden bench, it becomes an outdoor room—a wonderful place to congregate toward evening around the welcoming warmth of the fire.

Comfort, Pueblo-Style

When designing with an unconventional palette, let the materials work for you to create a house with personality.

Architect DANIEL HOFFMANN fell in love with the look and feel of Southwestern architecture when his parents moved to Santa Fe 30 years ago. When it came time for retirement, Daniel and his wife, Georgia, decided to make nearby Taos their new home. They found a site in town, just a half block from the historic district, and decided to design a home in the Pueblo style, using adobe bricks for walls and peeled logs for roof support. The native Pueblo Indians added rooms to their houses as they needed them, resulting in structures that appeared to have grown organically over time. Following the same approach, the Hoffmanns' house was planned as an assemblage of cubes rather than as a unified whole.

OPPOSITE The house has few interior doors, allowing long sight lines throughout to connect the main living spaces. Lowered beams are used to differentiate one room from another without obstructing the views. The sculpted wall between kitchen and dining areas, which mirrors the wall flanking the fireplace, hides the kitchen work area.

BELOW Located just half a block from the historic section of Taos, this home for a retired couple is built in the Pueblo style to look as if it had grown up over time.

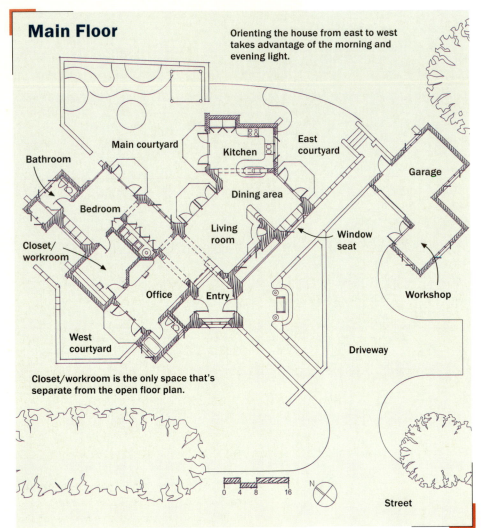

Main Floor

Orienting the house from east to west takes advantage of the morning and evening light.

Bathroom

Main courtyard

Kitchen

East courtyard

Garage

Dining area

Bedroom

Living room

Window seat

Closet/ workroom

Workshop

Office

Entry

West courtyard

Driveway

Closet/workroom is the only space that's separate from the open floor plan.

0 4 8   16

N

Street

Architect:
DWH Architects, Inc.

Builder:
Las Colonias Construction

Size: 1,985 sq. ft.

Location:
Taos, N. Mex.

Site and Light

Daniel wanted to make the most of the rare quality of the light in Taos, located atop a high mesa that allows light to enter almost horizontally at the start and end of the day. Since the street runs southeast to northwest, orienting the windows to the east and west also placed the house at a 45-degree angle to neighboring homes, which has the advantage of opening up longer views that don't look directly at the adjacent structures.

Because the building site has a drop of 7 ft. from one side to the other, the decision was made to sink the garage 4 ft. into the ground and to raise the master-bedroom wing 3 ft. above grade. In this way, all living spaces are kept at the same level. The adobe walls surrounding the courtyards provide privacy and help to disguise the height of the bedroom wing, while the sunken garage all but disappears from the street.

Open-Plan Living

Since it was just the two if them, Daniel and Georgia had few concerns about noise, so they chose to minimize the number of interior doors. They preferred a house that felt open, that allowed views from place to place, and that was all on one level for accessibility. Although they are both healthy and mobile

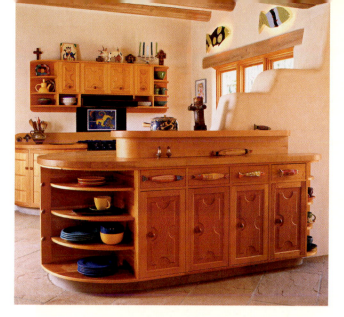

TOP To avoid the predictable monotony of banks of cabinet doors, upper kitchen cabinets were kept to a practical minimum, leaving room for open shelves and a broad expanse of windows.

ABOVE Oversized drawer pulls and hand-carved doors give the whole kitchen an air of crafted playfulness.

LEFT Two graceful archways frame a view from the entry to the window beyond. Without the window, the view would be far less welcoming. The antique desk is out of the way of the main living space, but its beauty can still be appreciated every day as the owners enter and leave the house.

Comfort, Pueblo-Style

The kitchen fits with the look and feel of the rest of the house—an important characteristic when building Not So Big.

today, they wanted to design a home they could stay in even if they became physically impaired.

Entering through the front door, you're greeted by a long view through two archways to a perfectly aligned window. The window is actually part of the master bedroom, but this is not apparent to a visitor. It simply looks like part of a graciously proportioned hallway. Without the window, the view would be much less appealing. The optical effect is to make the house look significantly larger than it really is—an important Not So Big concept.

The Hoffmanns wanted to make sure the kitchen blended in with the other living spaces, so they decided to minimize the number of upper cabinets, replacing what they could with windows and open shelving. A built-in wall pantry next to the refrigerator more than compensates for the lost storage space. The cabinet doors are custom carved, and the drawers have oversized pulls—painted wooden fish—created by a local artist. The refrigerator panel is also unique. Here, painted canvas has been stretched over the original black glass panel on one side. The result is a kitchen that looks more like living space than work space. And most important, it fits with the look and feel of the rest of the house—something to keep in mind when building Not So Big, where one space flows directly into the next.

The only space that isn't part of this open flow is a room originally intended as the master-bedroom closet. While the house was under construction, it occurred to Daniel and Georgia that, given its size, this space could really do double duty as a storage room for other things as well. They've dubbed this the Fibber McGee room, after the beloved 1930s radio character and his famous overstuffed closet. Here, the Hoffmanns store the supplies for their art and architecture projects. A large layout table in the center makes it an excellent "messy projects" room. Meanwhile, it works just fine as an everyday dressing room as well.

ABOVE AND LEFT Originally intended as a master-bedroom closet, the Fibber McGee room (named after the radio character who had a closet to end all closets) still stores clothes but also does double duty as a project room.

RIGHT The embracing wall of the beehive fireplace was sculpted to provide some separation between the sitting and dining areas. When you're seated in either space, your view is focused on the activity before you; but when you stand, the separation disappears as the wall steps back to reveal the adjacent room.

BELOW The window seat in the dining area has a lowered ceiling, making a wonderful sitting nook for one or two. It's connected to the kitchen visually but quite separate from the living room, thanks to the thick wing wall of the fireplace.

OPPOSITE The owner's home office opens off the skylit front foyer. The beamed opening between rooms has thickened walls at the base, making use of the sculptural quality of adobe. The desk is tucked neatly into an alcove with a lowered ceiling and similar beamed opening—a very comfortable place to work.

Adobe offers some wonderful opportunities for alcoves, wall niches, and creative storage.

Live-In Sculpture

The Hoffmanns' decision to build with native materials opened up some interesting design possibilities. Adobe, because of its thickness, offers some wonderful opportunities for alcoves, wall niches, and creative storage. Adobe walls were originally made of mud bricks reinforced with straw and were about 24 in. deep. Today the process is much the same, with bricks made to a standard 10-in. by 4-in. by 4-in. size. In this home, walls vary from 10 in. thick at walls without windows to 36 in. at the window seats. Once in place, the raw bricks can be sculpted with a pneumatic chipping tool. This is how the armrests on the window seats were made, as well as the stepped wing walls on either side of the beehive fireplace, the beveled openings surrounding the windows, and the bases of the beamed openings between rooms.

Lighting with a Personal Touch

*L*ighting can be an expensive part of a new home, but the Hoffmanns put Georgia's artistic flair to good use, saving a bundle in the process. All the wall sconces are simple porcelain fixtures, with wonderfully creative metal and wood shades made by the resident artist. This gives the house a highly personal touch, with walls adorned with everything from angels in the bedroom to fish in the kitchen. Lit from behind, these whimsical sculptures shine forth and make it eminently clear that this is the home of people who enjoy making their house a personal expression.

ABOVE The thickness of an adobe wall makes it possible to bury a deep cupboard into the wall. Known as an *alacena,* this is a typical feature of Pueblo architecture. The doors of the *alacena* match the kitchen cabinets, but with dancing gecko door pulls instead of fish. The owners haven't missed an opportunity to make everyday utility into a work of art.

Another traditional element in an adobe house is the *alacena,* a storage cupboard built into the wall much as we would set a medicine cabinet in place. But since adobe walls are so much thicker than the standard 2x4 walls we're used to, these cupboards can be almost 2 ft. deep. The Hoffmanns took advantage of this concept for their wood storage box adjacent to the fireplace. The doors, when closed, recall the motif of the kitchen cabinetry, integrating the two spaces.

When designing with an unconventional palette, as in this adobe example, you can explore the special characteristics of the materials and let them work for you to create a house with personality. Using the depth and sculptural qualities of adobe, as

LEFT Throughout the house, lighting is cleverly disguised as wall sculpture. Here, a wooden angel above the bed lights up at night to provide a soft glow for the master bedroom.

BELOW The view from the master bedroom extends across the courtyard to the mountains beyond.

well as the playful, informal feel that arises from the resulting softness of forms, the Hoffmanns have made a home that graciously invites you to stay a while. Just as the adobe walls extend from the front entry to the street in welcome, so the interiors wrap around its inhabitants and visitors in warm embrace. It may not look like a conventional home, but its comforts are traditional and inviting.

Thinking outside the Box

TODAY'S HOUSEHOLDS COME IN MANY different shapes and sizes, from blended families to separated ones, from couples with kids to individuals who choose to stay single. Rather than attempt to force all of them into the standard "three bedrooms up" house plan, it makes sense to rethink the house to fit the myriad needs of families, couples, and singles. This northern California home does just that. Designed for a specific situation, it is flexible enough to work in different ways according to changing circumstances.

Two small, separate houses allow for a variety of living arrangements.

When Fred and Barbara moved into the tiny concrete-block house on their new property in 1978, they were going through a difficult time in their marriage, and they knew that they would need some space to be apart. At the same time, they both wanted to be close to their three young children. They came up with an unusual solution: build a second house on the property, adjacent to the existing one (see the site plan on p. 128). Each adult would

(see the site plan on p. 128)

ABOVE Designed as a separate addition to a small existing house, the new house was built over a number of years by the owners themselves. Many of the construction materials were salvaged, including the big round-top window at the gable end, which became a focal point for the design.

OPPOSITE The clerestory windows, which capture the low south light in the winter months, are set in slightly from the end wall, allowing the form of the gable to be expressed. The round-top window is centered below the ridge of the gable, giving it a frame that completes the gable form. (PHOTO COURTESY JACOBSON SILVERSTEIN WINSLOW.)

ABOVE This east-facing window, salvaged from an old schoolhouse, allows light to stream into the bedroom each morning, a welcome to the day. It's trimmed differently than every other window in the house, the unadorned sash and mullions emphasizing its simplicity and beauty.

RIGHT This alcove just off the master bedroom, designed originally as a meditation space, now serves as a secluded desk nook, with a view onto the courtyard below. It's an ideal "place of one's own"—a tiny spot in the house just for one, to make of what you will.

live in one of the houses, and the children could move between them as they chose. Although this may seem like an uncommon solution to marital problems, Fred and Barbara were "thinking outside the box" of convention, creating an environment in which their children could flourish.

Working Together

Barbara, who is an architect, designed a house that would be simple to build. She also made extensive use of salvaged materials to keep costs down. Since Fred and Barbara did most of the construction themselves, they were able to collect materials gradually. Over time, they accumulated an assortment of found items: fir flooring that had once been siding on a military base, posts and beams from an old bridge, stair railings and treads, a schoolhouse window—literally everything but the kitchen sink. Though it took them many years to complete the construction, they were able to live on the site throughout the process, refining and embellishing as they went. And their salvaging, though labor intensive, paid big dividends, both in character added and money saved.

Once complete, the two small, separate houses allowed for a variety of living arrangements. When the couple needed time apart, there was a space for each of them, without it causing a major disruption to either their children's lives or their own. When the whole family wanted to get together, there were communal gathering spaces both inside the new house and out.

LEFT The area under a stairway is often unused or at best made into a closet. But the sloped ceiling below the stair can make a cozy corner for one or two chairs. Combined with a wood stove, as here, it becomes a warm spot to settle in on rainy days and in the evenings.

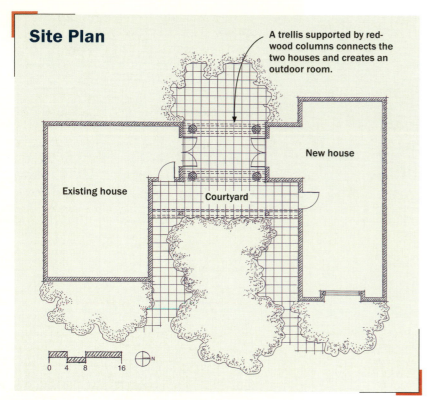

Site Plan

A trellis supported by red-wood columns connects the two houses and creates an outdoor room.

New house

Existing house

Courtyard

0 4 8   16   N

An Outdoor Room

To make a connection between the old house and the new, Barbara decided to create an outdoor room that would be defined much like any interior space, with a ceiling and four (implied) walls. The ceiling takes the form of a trellis, covered with wisteria and other flowering creepers that fill the connecting garden court-yard with year-round color. The walls are suggested by the four columns that support the beams above. Nothing more is required to make this a thoroughly de-lightful place and one of the most used "rooms" in the two houses.

In a Not So Big House, outdoor space can be just as important as indoor space, and it can be defined in the same ways: with alcoves, varying ceiling heights, con-necting views, and comfortable proportions. It benefits from thoughtfully designed and crafted details, such as the doubled rafters in this connecting trellis. And, when considered in conjunction with the interior of the house, the outdoor room can extend the living space into the surrounding landscape. This is easier to do in California than in a colder climate, but even in a less hospitable environment, a view of well-designed outdoor rooms can help make your perception of the house extend be-yond the walls.

ABOVE In near-perfect climates (with no bugs to speak of), French doors can be thrown open to allow interior and exterior spaces to flow together. A vine-entwined trellis blurs the distinction between inside and out, extending the sense of home into the surrounding landscape. (PHOTO COUR-TESY JACOBSON SILVERSTEIN WINSLOW.)

An outdoor room extends the living space into the surrounding landscape.

Doing Double Duty

The dining area in the new house was designed as the primary gathering spot for the family, but it also needed to work for entertaining. One of the keys to making a small house work is to make each space do double duty. If a space can be expanded or modified easily for an occasional use, you need to build only half as much space as if you were to build a separate room for each "once in a while" function.

Here, the dining area is close to the kitchen and to the French doors that open onto the arbored connection between the two houses, making it an inviting central location for the family to congregate. When guests come for dinner, the table can be extended all the way to the wood stove at the bottom of the stairs, allowing up to 20 people to be seated comfortably. For even larger gatherings, a long table can extend the full length of the house, from kitchen to living room. With such an open plan, there's a lot of flexibility for special occasions, yet each space still has its own definition.

The inglenook also does double duty. By day it's a cozy spot by the fire, the columns and half walls separating it psychologically— though not acoustically—from the main space. But when guests are visiting, this small alcove turns into a guest room with two beds. Wide drawers below the benches hold the neces-

LEFT The kitchen has few upper cabinets so there's room for a large window above the sink, which brings light and views into the work area. A spacious pantry serves the same function as cupboards, and a 4-ft.-long counter stores all the appliances: mixer, breadmaker, coffeemaker, and food processor. It's like a walk-in appliance garage.

BELOW The dining area, which works well for both everyday needs and larger gatherings, opens out onto the terrace beyond. A sheltering trellis bridges the two houses, creating an outdoor room with a wisteria ceiling. (PHOTO COURTESY JACOBSON SILVERSTEIN WINSLOW.)

When space is well designed, its special nooks and crannies can change function over time as the needs of family members change.

sary bedding. Though not completely private, it provides a comfortable sleeping place, with a bathroom conveniently nearby.

Another double-duty space is located on the upper level. The spacious master suite could readily be made into two bedrooms should the need arise. In its current configuration, it serves both as bedroom and adult retreat. When Barbara originally designed it, the south-facing alcove was intended as a meditation corner. Today it contains a desk and chair. Small spaces like this can change function as needed—from dressing area to in-home office to exercise room. When space is well designed, its special nooks and crannies can change function over time as the needs of family members change.

Weathering Change

Fred and Barbara's willingness to think outside the box to meet their family's housing needs has paid off. Their unusual design for living proved flexible enough to weather not only changes in their own family structure but also the inevitable changes that occur in all families with the passing of time. The two-house concept worked well while the children were growing up, and the arrangement continued even after Barbara and Fred's marriage ended. The original concrete-block house was ultimately turned over to the teenagers, and Barbara eventually moved away. The new house is now Fred's home, and when the kids—now fully grown—come to visit, the original house serves them as a guest house.

Although it's sometimes hard to admit that family life is not picture-perfect, when it's not, we need to find ways of designing that allow us to accommodate change gracefully over time. This is a wonderful example of a Not So Big House designed for the way this family really lived, with an unusual configuration that adapted readily as needs changed. It is impossible to predict how our lives will evolve, but if a house is well designed and built with materials that will last, it will mold easily to a new set of circumstances. An unconventional approach is often eminently sensible and will likely become more common as we tailor our homes to fit reality.

Architect: Jacobson Silverstein Winslow Architects

Builder: Fred Winslow

Size: 1,200 sq. ft. (new house)

Location: Lafayette, Calif.

Up Close

The head of the bed is set in a shallow window alcove with a low sloped ceiling. The windowsill is aligned with the top of the mattress. Although it's unusual to place a bed adjacent to a window, the views are wonderful, and provide a great connection with the outdoors. Just because an arrangement isn't typical doesn't mean you shouldn't do it.

Main Floor

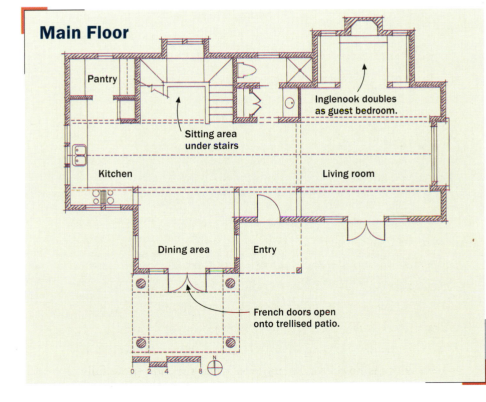

Pantry

Sitting area under stairs

Inglenook doubles as guest bedroom.

Kitchen

Living room

Dining area

Entry

French doors open onto trellised patio.

0 2 4 8 N

Upper Level

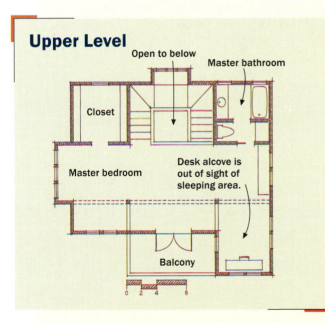

Open to below

Master bathroom

Closet

Master bedroom

Desk alcove is out of sight of sleeping area.

Balcony

0 2 4 8

Playfully
Sustainable

THE HOUSE THAT TED MONTGOMERY designed for his family near Burlington, Vermont, is an example of what's possible when you build with sustainability in mind. When you think of sustainable design—doing the right thing for the planet—you probably assume you have to settle for a house that's less than what you want: less waste, fewer luxuries (it's a bit like eating your vegetables). But Ted Montgomery wasn't willing to settle for less, and he designed a model of what's possible when you integrate a concern for energy efficiency with an irrepressible flair for invention.

The house is one of 13 in Ten Stones Intentional Community, a development in which people brought together their shared visions of home and neighborhood on 88 acres, 80 of which remain common open space. On their own half acre, Ted and wife Sarah tried a number of different locations and orientations for their home

ABOVE Designed as part of a community of 13 houses on 88 acres, the Montgomerys' home looks out onto the common green space. Together, homeowners decide how to use and manage the undeveloped acres. One decision was to sculpt a labyrinth into the grass.

OPPOSITE The garden room serves as a passive solar collector. Surrounding rooms have windows that open onto the space, allowing them to share in the warmth and the greenery year-round.

Combine invention, economy, beauty, and whimsy, and you have the ingredients for a really delightful place to live.

on paper before deciding on the current relationship between site, house, garage, and studio.

Because an energy-efficient house typically has few if any windows on the north face, Ted located the garage there, to buffer the main house from the north wind without compromising desirable window area. Originally the community had planned to have cars parked a distance away from the houses, but the cold, harsh reality of the Vermont winters changed some minds. So Ted instead disguised the garage by berming two sides with earth and adding a roof deck, which also offers a lookout over the community. In the spring, the sloped roof is planted with grass, further downplaying the garage.

ABOVE The siting of an energy-efficient house is critical. This house is oriented toward the sun, and the north and west sides are bermed (mounded with earth) to reduce the amount of wall surface exposed to the elements.

OPPOSITE In locating the house on the site, Ted wanted to minimize the number of trees cut down. The white ash that sprouts through the roof inspired the room that became the focus of the entire house.

A Room with a Viewpoint

One of Ted's goals was to minimize the number of trees that had to be cut down to make room for the house. He also wanted to ensure that it was oriented toward the sun. What evolved was a house designed around a passive solar sunspace—the garden room—with a 75-ft.-tall white ash growing through the middle of it. The trees that did have to be removed to make way for the house were milled into lumber that was used to finish the interior.

The garden room became the primary organizational focus for the house. The room is flooded with southern light, so it heats up over the course of a sunny winter day and acts as a passive solar collector. Ted placed all the main living spaces and bedrooms so they open onto this indoor-outdoor area. In this way, the garden room provides a major source of heat for the house.

The garden room itself opens onto an outdoor courtyard, created by the placement of the studio—Ted's workplace—at a 90-degree angle to the house. Just as interior spaces can be defined with two perpendicular walls to create a shelter around a specific activity, so too can exterior spaces. A beautiful trellislike gateway links the studio to the main house, adding further definition to the courtyard.

Up Close

An arched gateway between the house (left) and the studio marks the entry into the south-facing courtyard. This intriguing opening between buildings welcomes visitors and offers a glimpse of the surprises this house has in store. (PHOTO COURTESY TED MONTGOMERY.)

Connecting Views

As soon as you step inside the house, you know it'll be a fun place to spend time. No matter where you are in the house, there are long views through the space, which gives an airy, spacious feel to the 1,200-sq.-ft. main level. When you look at the floor plan, you can see that the entryway, living area, dining area, and kitchen are all open to one another, yet they are clearly identified as separate places by the walls that define them.

This is a key to making Not So Big feel bigger without losing a sense of intimacy and comfort. Connect activity areas with views from one place to the next, but don't make the space so undifferentiated that it all looks and feels the same. In the Montgomerys' home, the variety of shapes the space takes, the connecting views, and the feast of color and pattern make this a home that really works. Here, invention has been substituted for scale, to make a house that draws you in and invites you to take a second look.

LEFT Long diagonal views connect all the main living spaces, making the house appear larger than it really is. The view here is from the kitchen to the living room.

Architect:
Indiana Architecture
& Design

Builder:
Ted Montgomery

Size: 2,300 sq. ft.

Location:
Burlington, Vt.

Connect activity areas with views from one place to the next, but don't make the space so undifferentiated that it all looks and feels the same.

Main Floor

Garage buffers the house from north wind.

Mudroom

Garage

View from entry connects all main living spaces.

Living room

Entry

Dining area

Window seat

Master bathroom

Kitchen

Shower

Master bedroom

Tree

Garden room

Trellised gateway

Studio

Courtyard

All main living spaces open onto the garden room.

N

0   4   8   16

ABOVE The shower in the master bathroom, lined on the walls with recycled plastic instead of tile to facilitate cleaning, is wheelchair accessible. The house's copper motif continues in the towel bar at right.

Making Magic with Materials

The interior of the house is filled with unique details, created with a sense of whimsy that fills the house with a lightness of spirit. Ted made most of the cabinetry and modular furniture himself out of plywood and Medite, a formaldehyde-free particleboard, that he painted with nontoxic paint. The couches pull apart into individual chairs, with storage for magazines and papers built into the backs. The furniture's bright colors and whimsical cutouts add a playfulness that's in keeping with the informality of the house. The same is true of the door panels on the front of the two pantry cupboards, which sport a motif evocative of Swiss cheese and soap bubbles (see the photo on p. 136). Who says you can't have fun with design?

The Energy-Efficient House

No matter where you live, it's important to design with energy efficiency in mind. What that means, however, varies depending on your location. Understanding which strategies are appropriate for your region and climate requires some careful homework. During the energy crisis of the 1970s, many books and articles were written on harnessing naturally occurring energy sources like the sun and the wind. Unfortunately, not all strategies were appropriate for all places, and many houses were built with energy-efficient features that simply didn't work for their particular climate.

In a northern climate like Vermont's, the winters are long and cold, and the sun is intermittent. Given such conditions, a south-facing passive-solar sunspace is one of the best ways to capture the available heat. When the space warms from the sun's rays, windows between the house and the sunspace can be opened to heat the home's interior; on cloudy days, the sunspace simply acts as a buffer, providing welcome relief from the snowy vistas beyond.

In areas with plenty of winter sunshine and less extreme temperatures, a more direct approach makes sense. By facing most of the windows to the south, the sun enters the living spaces and warms the interior without the need for a sunspace buffer.

Whether or not you employ passive-solar features, the most important strategy in building energy efficiently is to do an excellent job of insulating and controlling air infiltration. This is true even in hot climates. Instead of using insulation to keep the heat in, you're using it to keep the heat out. And to keep cooling loads to a minimum, windows need to be located to minimize solar gain during the months when air temperatures are above the comfort range.

When a house is built tightly to minimize air infiltration, there's one additional energy-efficient feature that's crucial. An air-to-air heat exchanger is a device that automatically introduces fresh air into the house while retrieving the heating or cooling energy of the outgoing air. This can save about 85 percent of the heating or air-conditioning energy and helps avoid problems with stagnant air and poor indoor air quality. All new houses that need heating or cooling systems should have air-to-air heat exchangers. It's a matter of health and not something to be left out. Insist on it.

ABOVE Creative storage ideas are evident throughout the house. In the typically little-used area below the bed, the owner has made storage chests on rollers for books and treasures.

LEFT The bathroom countertop is made of copper, a long-lasting, relatively inexpensive surface that will weather and age beautifully over time. The sheet copper is wrapped around a 1½–in. layer of plywood.

The kitchen-island countertop is made from one of the ash trees felled on the site, and the rest of the countertops are made of plywood covered with copper sheeting, which ages beautifully over time and costs about the same as plastic laminate. Copper is also used in the stair railing but in tubular form. Reminiscent of the Art Nouveau style, it's a work of art in its own right. The towel bars in the bathroom continue the copper motif. The floors on the main level are concrete that has been colored with an acid-based stain to make it look like mottled leather.

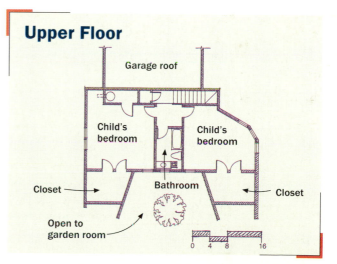

Upper Floor

Garage roof

Child's bedroom

Child's bedroom

Closet

Bathroom

Closet

Open to garden room

0 4 8 16

*You can create the effect
of an expensive built-in using
inexpensive materials.*

Another material that's used creatively throughout the house is paint. Instead of making all the walls the same color and using moldings or wood trim to decorate each space, Ted used color to provide visual interest. By layering an element of one color over a surface of another color, you can create the effect of an expensive built-in using inexpensive materials. In the living-room bookshelves, for example, the back wall is painted purple while the shelves themselves, made of plywood, are green. This makes the room appear larger and the overall composition more interesting.

Although there's a lot to take in here, the number of basic materials used is surprisingly small. This limitation of the palette is key. By being innovative with each element, you can make a house that has a lot going on without becoming overwhelming. There's a fine line between whimsy and cacophony.

What is most impressive about this house, though, is the apparent ease with which it brings together considerations of sustainability, energy efficiency, playfulness, and comfort. The effortlessness is deceptive. To design and build a home that integrates so many concepts in a way that looks natural requires significant skill. This is the art of good design. Combine invention, economy, beauty, and whimsy, and you have the ingredients for a really delightful place to live.

OPPOSITE **Materials and color are used creatively throughout the house. Built-ins are made of plywood painted with nontoxic paints. The couch is designed to be pulled apart into individual chairs to seat a crowd, with storage built into the backs.**

Up Close

Copper tubing is used in the stair-railing design to turn an everyday necessity into a work of art.

One Phase at a Time

FOR SEVERAL YEARS AFTER THEY found the perfect property on the shores of Maine's Penobscot Bay, Stephanie and Sandy couldn't bring themselves to build on the land because it had such a raw magnificence. But camping with two small children eventually lost its charm, and they realized that without a house to come home to, their opportunities to enjoy the site were limited. So they asked architect Robert Knight to design them a low-impact house that would initially serve as a vacation home and, over time, become their year-round residence. With two children, they knew that once they moved into the house full-time, they would need more bedrooms, but that was still in the future. They weren't sure exactly what they would need when the time came, so they decided to build the house in two phases.

Building in phases is a basic principle when designing Not So Big. So often, in an attempt to see into the future, houses are

Building in phases is a basic principle when designing Not So Big.

ABOVE With such a magnificent piece of property, the owners wanted a house that was unobtrusive and had a low impact on the land.

OPPOSITE The second-floor landing is both circulation space and closet, utilizing the normally unused area under the eaves. Above the door, transom windows extend to the ceiling, giving a continuous flow to the space. Make these areas solid and the house would feel smaller and more closed in.

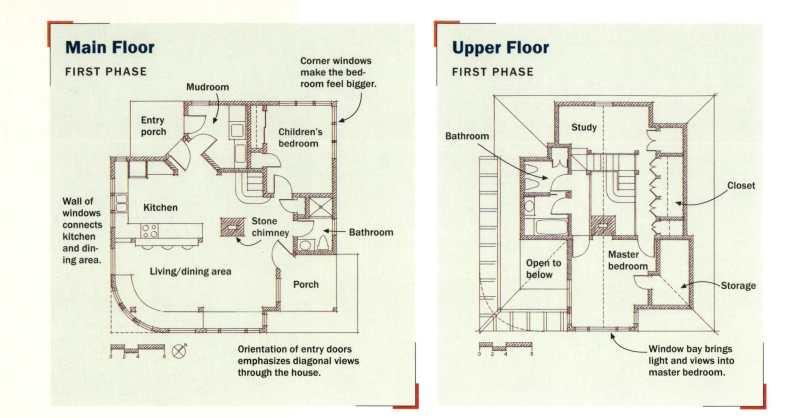

Main Floor

FIRST PHASE

- Mudroom
- Entry porch
- Corner windows make the bedroom feel bigger.
- Children's bedroom
- Wall of windows connects kitchen and dining area.
- Kitchen
- Stone chimney
- Bathroom
- Living/dining area
- Porch

0 2 4 8 ⊗ N

Orientation of entry doors emphasizes diagonal views through the house.

Upper Floor

FIRST PHASE

- Bathroom
- Study
- Closet
- Open to below
- Master bedroom
- Storage

0 2 4 8

Window bay brings light and views into master bedroom.

ABOVE The first phase of the design was an almost square, 1,400-sq.-ft. house with a hip roof and lots of windows and skylights to bring in the light and views. (PHOTO COURTESY ROBERT PERRON.)

overdesigned and overbuilt for circumstances that never come to pass or that are radically different than imagined at the start of a project. Phasing allows you to build what you need now and add on only when you fully understand your new needs.

Bob Knight designed a house that was quite compact, with just 900 sq. ft. of finished space on the main level and 520 sq. ft. on the upper level—an ideal vacation retreat, with an informal floor plan and lots of windows to take in the breathtaking views. The house site was selected to minimize the number of trees that would have to be cut down, while still allowing views of the water and the tidal flats to the southeast. Stephanie and Sandy knew they would add a gabled wing onto the north side of the house in the future, and Bob simply designed the original house with that in mind, postponing any formal plans for the addition until the need arose.

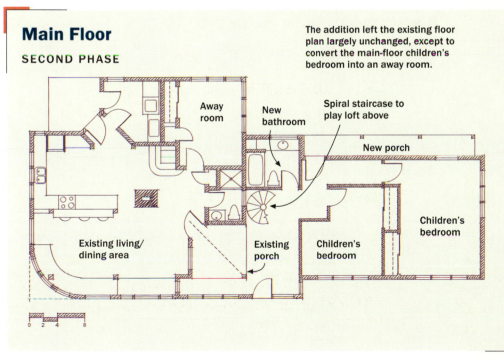

Main Floor

SECOND PHASE

The addition left the existing floor plan largely unchanged, except to convert the main-floor children's bedroom into an away room.

Away room

New bathroom

Spiral staircase to play loft above

New porch

Existing living/ dining area

Existing porch

Children's bedroom

Children's bedroom

0 2 4 8

ABOVE The addition, built 12 years after the original house, added bedrooms and a bathroom for the children but left the heart of the original floor plan untouched. The house works just as well as a year-round residence as it did as a vacation home.

Architect:
Knight Associates

Builder:
Stewart Construction

Size: 1,420 sq. ft. (original house); 930 sq. ft. (addition)

Location:
Penobscot Bay, Maine

We live in our homes much more informally than most standard floor plans would suggest.

When they did, in fact, add on some 12 years later, the new wing included bedroom and bathroom space for the kids but little else. The main part of the house, the informal living space, turned out to be as perfect for year-round living as it was for vacationing. This highlights the fact that our homes today can learn a lot from how we live when we're "officially relaxing"—we live in our homes much more informally than most standard floor plans would suggest. Despite the fact that they were transforming a casual vacation place into a year-round home, Stephanie and Sandy saw no reason to add a formal dining or living area. They knew how they lived in the house and how they entertained there. It was the informality that made them feel comfortable, and their friends enjoyed this aspect of the design just as much as they did.

Taking the Long View

The plan itself is very simple—basically a square covered by a hipped roof, with two corners removed, one for the front entry and one for the deck, with the roof extending down to shelter these two spaces. The front entry and porch doors are oriented at a 45-degree angle to the rest of the floor plan, emphasizing a diagonal view through the house. The views within the house are also mainly on the diagonal, which makes the house feel larger than it actually is. It's an important trick in making Not So Big feel bigger. You can sit in the dining area, for example, and look back past the wood stove to the stairway; or you can be

working in the kitchen and look out through the living-area window to the ocean beyond.

The corner windows in the dining area and the main-floor bedroom are further elaborations on this motif. When you take away the visual solidity of the outside corner of a room by replacing a wall with windows, the room feels significantly bigger, provided there's an open view beyond. It's as though the great outdoors becomes part of the room itself.

Rooms to Live In

In this home, the eating area—with its window seats, corner windows, and skylights—is such a wonderful place to be that the living room takes a subordinate role. This is where people gather, and with the table extended, it can accommodate a large party if necessary. The kitchen counter is raised 6 in. on the dining side, which allows family and friends to socialize with the cook during meal preparation and has the added benefit of hiding the kitchen mess while people are eating. Many people hesitate to give up a formal dining room because of concerns about looking at dirty dishes. This organization of space eliminates that problem. Why build two eating areas when you can have one extra-

ABOVE The wall of windows with skylights above, connecting the kitchen and dining area, seems to float past the work space. Defined by the lower wood ceiling and corner column, the kitchen is wide open yet still distinct—almost like a house within a greenhouse.

OPPOSITE By raising the counter between the kitchen and eating area, dirty dishes are hidden from the table. With no walls to separate the kitchen from the living areas, the whole main level benefits from the easy informality of the light-filled kitchen hub.

ABOVE The master bedroom is relatively small, but the visual connection with the landing through the upper transoms gives it a feeling of spaciousness. The stonework of the chimney provides a wonderful contrast in texture to the rest of the room.

RIGHT A window bay brings the view of woods, water, and sky right into the master bedroom. Though the alcove is small in terms of square footage, its impact is great.

ordinary one that brings you pleasure every day and delights your guests as well?

When the addition was built, the first-floor bedroom, which had previously served as the kids' bunk room, was turned into an away room. This space, near the main social areas of the house, lets adults get some work done or make a quiet phone call without separating themselves completely from family activities. Some people prefer to install a French door, so a room like this one can also serve as a place for noisier activities like television or video games—to be isolated acoustically but not visually. Children often want to be close to the adults but don't want to do the same things. This simple solution can avoid a lot of irritation caused by competing activities and the high-decibel levels that generally go along with kids.

A Simple Stack of Stones

A powerful aspect of the design is the spectacular stone chimney that extends directly up through the center of the house, creating impressive views from every angle. This is an excellent example of how craftsmanship can enhance a home. Initially, the house had been designed to have a brick chimney, which hadn't been thought of as a "statement piece." However, Stephanie and Sandy found a local stone mason, Jeff Gamelin, who could work magic with the stones found on local beaches. Although it is essentially just a straight, square assemblage of stones, his work transcends the medium, and the chimney becomes

> *"When you start with a smaller area and then really finish it beautifully, you end up with a far better place to live."*

the focal point of the house, both upstairs and down.

This is the kind of craftsmanship that makes a Not So Big House special. Thanks in large part to the conscious decision made at the beginning of this project to minimize its impact on the land, the house itself was kept small, and the money that would have otherwise gone into square footage went instead into quality of craft and materials. With all the wood and stone in the house, it's not inexpensive per square foot. But if you have only 1,400 sq. ft., it's still within a reasonable price range. As Bob Knight says, "When you start with a smaller area and then really finish it beautifully, you end up with a far better place to live."

Up Close

A stone chimney can be so much more than just a pile of rocks. In this chimney, made from local beach stones, craft becomes art, bringing beauty to almost every room in the house. The tiny built-in niche halfway up the chimney provides an opportunity to display a treasured object.

LEFT Skylights are sometimes referred to as roof windows, yet they're seldom located in such a way that they really act as windows—places that allow access to both light and view. When you have a steeply sloped roof, as in this house, locating the skylight's sill below ceiling level gives you all the benefits of a normal window in an area that would normally require a dormer to access the view.

Updating a Not So Big House

ABOVE The original house, built in 1982, was designed to be initially inexpensive, with remodeling planned for the future. In 1999, when the remodeling was done, the outside remained essentially the same, but the inside was transformed from "builder basic" to designer detailed. (PHOTO COURTESY DAVID OTTENSTEIN.)

Barry katz caught on to the idea of building Not So Big early. As the owner of a high-end, custom homebuilding company, he'd seen what can happen when homeowners spend all their money on square footage and volume. He was all too familiar with the bigger-is-better philosophy of the '80s—and with houses where one or more rooms remain unused, often even unfurnished, for years after construction is complete. This just didn't make sense to him, so for his own family he chose a very different approach. Barry and his wife, Susan, found a site they liked within walking distance of downtown Westport, Connecticut, Susan's hometown. They asked New Haven architect Barry Svigals to help them design a house that they could build with their limited budget and later remodel to include more bells and whistles as finances allowed.

To save on expensive square footage, the house they built in 1982 had no separate formal spaces. When friends came to visit, they were welcomed into the family's living area, where the

The remodeling didn't require the addition of a lot more space, but what already existed clearly needed to be redefined.

OPPOSITE The remodeled living room works better than it did before, even though it is technically smaller. A 10-ft.-high ceiling replaces the original cathedral ceiling, making the room more intimate. If a space feels comfortable, it's much more likely to be lived in, even if it doesn't look as dramatic.

Main Floor

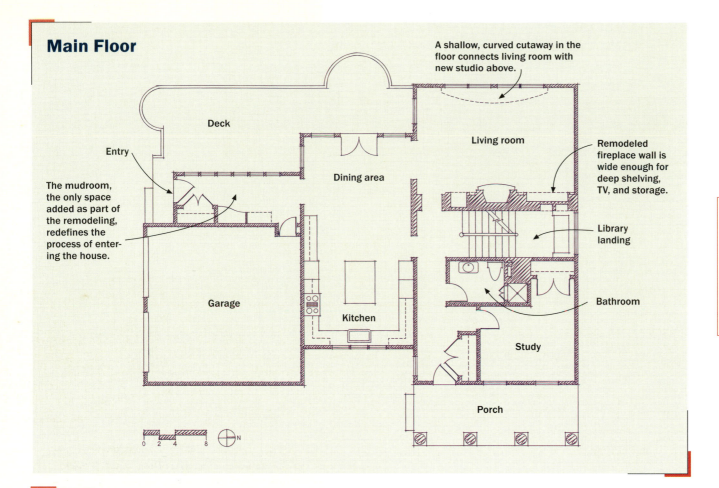

A shallow, curved cutaway in the floor connects living room with new studio above.

Deck

Entry

The mudroom, the only space added as part of the remodeling, redefines the process of entering the house.

Dining area

Living room

Remodeled fireplace wall is wide enough for deep shelving, TV, and storage.

Library landing

Garage

Kitchen

Bathroom

Study

Porch

0 2 4 8 N

Architect:
Svigals Associates
Builder:
Barry Katz Homebuilding
Size: 2,700 sq. ft.
Location:
Westport, Conn.

Upper Floor

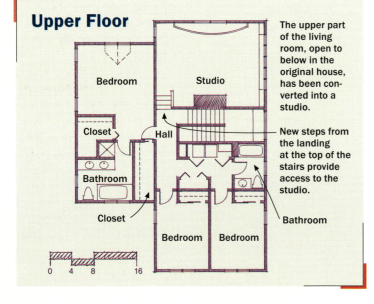

Bedroom

Studio

Closet

Hall

Bathroom

Closet

Bedroom

Bedroom

Bathroom

The upper part of the living room, open to below in the original house, has been converted into a studio.

New steps from the landing at the top of the stairs provide access to the studio.

0 4 8 16

kitchen, dining room, and living room were open to one another. The finishing details, which Barry and Susan knew they would eventually want to upgrade, began as inexpensive builder standards. With his building background, Barry Katz knew that changing the interior structure and adding windows would be prohibitively expensive if done later. So the couple spent the money they saved on square footage and expensive millwork to fill the house with light and to make rooms that would be big enough to be comfortable even when their two young children were strapping teens. In many ways, you could say that they built a Not So Big starter house.

Fast forward 15 years. The money for more details and refinements is available, and it's time to remodel. Barry and Susan again called Barry Svigals, and together they evolved a plan for the remodeling. The basic house still served the functions of family living just fine. But now Susan needed an in-home office; an ever-expanding collection of books was spilling from their makeshift shelves; and there was an overflow of coats, hats, shoes, and pet supplies, all without a home. The remodeling didn't require the addition of a lot more space, but what already existed clearly needed to be redefined.

One Room Becomes Two

One feature of the original house that Barry and Susan found less attractive than they'd expected was the cathedral ceiling in the living room. Although it looked impressive, it made the room uncomfortable to sit in. They always felt as if they were on display

ABOVE The upper section of the cathedral-ceilinged living room was converted into a studio, with a curved cutout and railing that opens up the studio to the living room below. The windows in the gable end wall remained unchanged, and both levels now benefit from the light and view they provide.

LEFT Extra windows, like this round top in the master bedroom, were included in the original design to fill the house with light. Even though the budget was limited, the owners knew how much more expensive it would be to add these elements later.

when they were in the room, because the shape of the space made it seem very formal. Even when guests were over, it didn't function very well, because the high ceiling turned the room into an echo chamber.

Svigals's solution was to turn the upper part of the room into a studio for Susan, accessible by four new steps from the landing at the top of the stairs. To avoid the need for a major redesign of the west facade, the window configuration was left intact, with a shallow opening and railing connecting the study with the living room below, allowing both to benefit from the light and view.

Now that the remodeling's done, Barry and Susan find that the living room is a far more comfortable room to be in—both for the family and when guests are over. The remodeled room has a 10-ft.-high ceiling, so it's by no means a low space, but it is no longer an echoing cavern. Best of all, the cutaway to the studio is a beautiful form, intriguing to visitors, and a graceful way to let in light.

ABOVE The only addition to the remodeled house is a mudroom, connected to the dining area with a pocket door. Rather than use a door that's solid and impenetrable, this one is made of translucent glass, which lets in the light but not the view.

RIGHT A small desk surface just around the corner from the mudroom door provides a place for mail sorting, menu planning, and family scheduling. The pigeonhole slots above allow mail to be sorted on the spot, before the piles form.

OPPOSITE When a mudroom is the family's everyday entry, it deserves to be more than just a space to store coats and shoes. With a wall of windows, this new mudroom is a wonderful light-filled transition space between outside and in. The bench is a great place to sit and take off muddy shoes, and its curve is echoed in the soffit above, adding a playful touch. There's even a lookout post for the canine welcoming committee.

An Everyday Entry

The only space added as part of the remodeling was the mudroom, which runs the length of the garage and brings you into the dining area through a translucent pocket door. Because this would be their primary entrance into the house, Barry and Susan wanted it to be a cheery place. A Not So Big House should not only welcome guests but also family members—if they enter through a back door, that's where the design effort needs to be. By making the west wall of the mudroom entirely

out of windows, this space is constantly bathed with light. There are places for all the outside gear, the pet supplies (and the pet), and a general message board. And when the Katzes step through the door into the dining area, they already feel at home.

Compare this to the earlier entry process. They used to move directly from the garage into the kitchen, with no transition space—an unsettling experience. There was no place to take off coats, and perhaps more important, no place to be received by the house before entering the family realm. Whether it's a mudroom or a small vestibule that helps make the transition, when such a space exists, it's as though the house greets you. This space serves far more than just a practical function. It's the spatial equivalent of the family's welcome mat.

Bookshelves and Built-Ins

The Katzes had managed to acquire a small library of books since they'd built the original house in 1982, and they wanted to add plenty of built-in shelving to accommodate the ever-growing collection. When you're a book lover, every available surface must be considered for shelving. It's important to be creative when you are looking at wall surfaces to find places where your shelves will be well integrated and add character to the space. It helps, in fact, if you think of books as extra-thick wallpaper.

ABOVE Space was borrowed from the reconfigured wall between the stairway and the living room to create additional shelves for the owners' growing collection of books. The built-in couch at the landing, with ample cushions and reading light, is a wonderful place to sit and read.

OPPOSITE The owners worked with an interior designer to create this wall of shelves. By building the shelves 4 in. out from the wall surface, the painting above the fireplace has a framed, inset appearance and space is made for the full depth of the television.

Many landing nooks look appealing but don't get used. This one is big enough and inviting enough that it really does work.

Svigals suggested that they take the wall opening that formerly overlooked the living room and make it into a library wall. Barry and Susan were initially hesitant about making the change, but they now agree that the new library landing is a wonderful addition. When combined with the built-in couch (with its own swing-arm reading light), it provides a great spot to curl up with a good book. Many landing nooks look appealing but don't get used. This one is big enough and inviting enough that it really does work.

Bookshelves were added in other places, too. In Susan's new studio, a double row of shelves runs the length of the north wall, under a new row of small windows (see the photo on p. 155). The windows have a head height of 4 ft. 6 in., just right for someone sitting at the desk. Both the windows and the bookshelves are lower than normal to encourage you to sit down and see them at comfortable eye level. When there's a low kneewall, as here, employing such strategies can make the space both more usable and more comfortable.

In the living room, the whole fireplace wall has been made into shelving and storage, with places for books, CDs, tapes, and audio/video equipment. The wall itself has been thickened substantially (to 24 in.) to make room for the television and the lower cabinets. Although this makes the room slightly smaller in terms of usable square footage, you barely

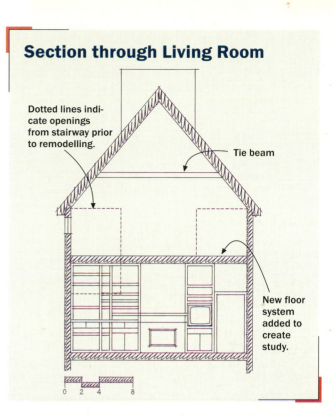

Section through Living Room

Dotted lines indicate openings from stairway prior to remodelling.

Tie beam

New floor system added to create study.

0 2 4 8

notice the difference in a room this size. People are often loath to give up floor space for storage, yet the result is a more functional and more beautiful room. In a Not So Big House, the built-ins are designed to do more with less. They become works of art in themselves, and the room is far more useful with them in it.

An Old-World Look

Barry and Susan had been collecting ideas and clipping pictures from design magazines for years, and when it came time to remodel, they put them to good use. They both loved the traditional detailing that gives a house a sense of permanence and the feeling that it was built in an earlier era. Trimwork is one of the key details that has changed significantly over the years, becoming narrower and less detailed. But just because a house is new doesn't mean it has to use today's standard moldings. Throughout the newly remodeled house, the moldings are suggestive of a house that's much older, and the kitchen and bathrooms have the kind of detailing typical of the end of the 1800s. It's details like these that give a house its personality, telling you a lot about what's important to the people who live there.

When you design a starter house with future remodeling in mind, you can initially keep detailing and its associated costs to a minimum, while children are young and elegant surfaces are in danger of being damaged. A decade later, when the kids have outgrown the desire to color on the wallpaper and you're ready to remodel, there's usually more money available to personalize the house. In the meantime, collecting design and decorating ideas is an excellent way to keep the vision of your dream house alive and well. And the result, like the Katzes' home, will be a truly delightful, eminently comfortable, and better-than-ever Not So Big House.

Instead of a combination refrigerator/freezer unit, the owners opted for a larger refrigerator and located freezer drawers in the island. When the drawers are closed, you'd never suspect they were anything other than regular cabinetry.

Just because a house is new doesn't mean it has to use today's standard moldings.

ABOVE Just because a house is new doesn't mean it has to look it. Here, everything from the floor tile and high wainscoting to the faucets and built-in medicine cabinets has been lovingly detailed to look like a bathroom from an earlier era. In its earlier incarnation, the finishes in this room were standard 1980s fare.

Tight Quarters

THE IDEA OF BUILDING SMALLER and better houses strikes a chord with people in many parts of the country because they recognize that just having a lot of space doesn't necessarily make a place feel like home. But in a large city like New York, the issues are a little different. Here, almost everyone lives in a space that's tiny and cramped, and you don't consciously decide to build small—the decision is made for you. The idea of building Not So Big is a perfect fit for city spaces. As architect Josh Heitler, owner of a 560-sq.-ft. co-op apartment in East Soho, puts it, "You're always up against the challenge of a limited amount of space, so you're always looking for tricks to make something look and feel bigger."

When you focus on ideas per square foot rather than on dollars per square foot, you find you can live more comfortably in less space.

RIGHT An old medical-office cabinet stripped of its original paint provides additional storage space in the kitchen. Using a stand-alone piece rather than built-in cabinetry keeps the old brick wall uncluttered, thus adding a feeling of spaciousness.

BELOW In older apartments there are often challenges to work around, such as the plumbing stacks for the building, which run up through the thick wall between the dresser and the bed. A gas meter adjacent to the window is cleverly disguised behind a hanging mirror that can be moved aside when the meter reader calls.

When Josh purchased the apartment in the summer of 1997, it was in a sad state of repair. The space was dark, with a tiny bathroom and kitchen monopolizing the two windows at one end of the 50-ft.-long space. The floor was covered with layer upon layer of carpet and linoleum, the edges peeling up to expose the old flooring below. When Josh invited his mother to come and see his new home, she burst into tears. Clearly this was not the future she'd had in mind for her son.

When a space looks this inhospitable, it takes some imagination to see its potential. But Josh had just completed his architectural training and had done his thesis on adaptive reuse, which is all about making older buildings serve new functions in innovative ways. His new residence gave him the opportunity to test some of his theories.

Down to the Bare Bones

The first step was to gut the place. Everything was stripped down to the studs and the original floor boards. The floor had a noticeable slope from side to side, so Josh decided to level it out with a new 2x4 floor-joist system set on top of the existing surface. He liked the character of the old structure, though, so he decided to leave at least one area with both the floor boards and ceiling joists exposed. He also liked the texture of the brick wall that ran the length of the apartment and opted to leave this as it was, making it a key feature of the new design.

If you move from a small area into a larger area, you subconsciously compare the two and feel the relative spaciousness of the larger one.

To make the most of the four existing windows for the primary living spaces, Josh wanted to relocate the kitchen and bathroom to the middle of the apartment. However, when you're redesigning within the confines of an apartment block, you have to tie into the existing vertical plumbing runs and vent stacks, which limit your options for relocation. Josh figured he could run the new pipes underneath the slightly raised floor he'd planned, but the toilet was a major limiting factor. It had to have sufficient slope to the main vertical sewer pipe and to the vent stack. So the first floor-plan decision, and one that dictated the layout of much of the rest of the apartment, was the location of the toilet. Once this was determined, everything else fell into place.

Extending the View

If Josh hadn't made the effort to place the rooms needing less natural light in the narrow middle section of the apartment, the overall design would have been far less inviting. Locating the two main rooms at either end of the space and allowing the full extent of the long brick wall to be visible throughout the apartment creates the impression that the space is much larger than it actually is. When you can see a full 50 ft. of unobstructed view, your mind tells you this is a big space, even when it's only 10 ft. wide.

Architect:
Lacina Group, Architects

Builder:
Josh Heitler and JK Remodeling

Size: 560 sq. ft.

Location: New York, N.Y.

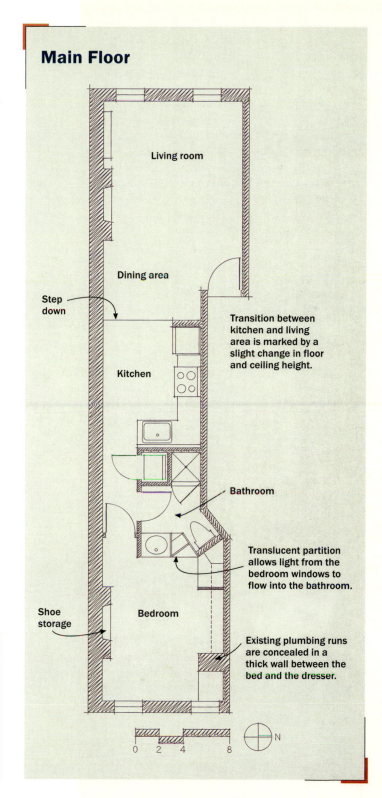

Main Floor

Living room

Dining area

Step down

Kitchen

Transition between kitchen and living area is marked by a slight change in floor and ceiling height.

Bathroom

Translucent partition allows light from the bedroom windows to flow into the bathroom.

Shoe storage

Bedroom

Existing plumbing runs are concealed in a thick wall between the bed and the dresser.

0 2 4 8

N

RIGHT The mirror above the sink stands in for the window you'd typically find in this location; its reflection provides a view of the living-room windows. Mirrors can be used creatively like this to bring daylight into areas that would otherwise be dark or far from outdoor views.

Up Close

Because the fireplace in the bedroom no longer works, it has been put to new use as a place to store shoes. When you are designing Not So Big, any nook or cranny—whatever its original purpose—is fair game for creative reuse.

The layout also breaks the apartment into three distinct zones. The narrower center zone is more compressed, while the larger rooms at either end create a sense of release. This is a technique that architects use frequently to increase the sense of size. If you move from a small area into a larger area, you subconsciously compare the two and feel the relative spaciousness of the larger one. When this is combined with a change in floor or ceiling height, the experience is further enhanced. Even though the difference in height between the kitchen and the living room is only a matter of a few inches, perceptually the effect is dramatic, and the 12-ft. by 14-ft. living room seems significantly larger as a result.

Weaving Old and New

When space and natural light are restricted, it's critical to give the interiors some vitality. You can do this with expensive materials and special details, but when money is limited, you have to be more creative. Josh's research into adaptive reuse had brought

home the fact that if you can lay bare some of the original building materials, they add a character and quality that new construction simply doesn't possess—and they're essentially free, because they're already in place. Still, some new construction was obviously going to be needed to accommodate the practical necessities, such as cooking, bathing, and storage. So Josh combined the old with the new, keeping the design spare to create a contemporary look and keep costs to a minimum.

Rather than attempt to make the old materials look new or the new materials match the character of the old, the two stand in distinct contrast to one another, giving the apartment a more animated spirit than if it were composed of either one alone. The kitchen, for example, has a smooth white ceiling and tile floor—all new materials—while the living room shows off the original joists and floor boards, which gives that space a very different quality and visual weight. It's more rustic, more textured, and it allows you to experience the full breadth of the space—from one side to the other and right up to the rafters. This is another trick used by architects and designers to make a small space feel bigger. As Josh describes it, "If there's a place where you can see the measure of the whole space, it can make an enormous difference and greatly increase the sense of scale."

LEFT Even the area over the bed has been used to provide extra storage. This shelf has standard under-cabinet lights—the kind you'd normally find in a kitchen—attached to the bottom, which serve as reading lights.

BELOW Suspending the bookshelves from the wall leaves the floor area of the living room fully visible, making it appear larger. Limiting the amount of furniture and placing the television on a rollaway cart helps this small room feel ample rather than cramped.

Dining in the Big Apple

In New York, space is at enough of a premium that many apartments have no eating area at all. The living room often serves as the dining room as well, with plates set on the coffee table or perched on laps. Another common solution in a tiny living space is to have an equally tiny table set in the kitchen, with just enough room to get to the refrigerator and stove. Josh didn't like either of these alternatives, so he did something that might initially seem to be a waste of space. Instead of extending the kitchen cabinetry all the way to the end of the wall, he held it back a couple of feet. Then he placed the dining table along the long brick wall, just beyond the break between the kitchen and living room, and thus a few inches lower than the kitchen.

There was in fact just enough room for the table in the kitchen, but moving it into the living room like this gives it quite a different personality. Its separation from other activity areas is accentuated by the step down from the kitchen and the drywall enclosure around the living-room fireplace. The composition of this tiny dining area shows how little is required to create a sense of shelter around activity. Take away its boundaries, and it's just a table in a hallway.

ABOVE The dining area is defined on the left by the change in floor and ceiling height from the adjacent kitchen area and on the right by the enclosure for the fireplace. The pool of light created by the hanging lamp further accentuates the sense that this is a separate place, with its own distinct personality.

Through the Looking Glass

Although there are no windows in the middle zone of the house, there's still plenty of natural light. Josh used mirrors and interior windows to borrow light for areas that would otherwise be dark and unwelcoming.

In the kitchen, instead of the typical window above the sink, he placed a mirror that reflects the windows at the end of the living room. He can still see outside, even though his back is turned to the exterior wall.

Instead of building a standard, solid wall between the bedroom and the bathroom, Josh installed a translucent membrane that allows light from the bedroom windows to flood the bathroom as well. The mirror above the bathroom sink has a matching mirror on the bedroom side, which reflects additional light into the bedroom.

That such a long, thin space should seem so light filled and airy is a testament to the inventiveness of its architect. To have accomplished this on a shoestring budget is even more impressive. When you look at this truly tiny living space and see all the amenities it provides, it's easy to see that what our homes are really lacking isn't space, it's inventiveness. When you focus on ideas per square foot rather than on dollars per square foot, you find you can live more comfortably in less space.

BELOW Because access to daylight is so limited in this long, narrow space, the bathroom wall is made of Plexiglas rather than studs and wallboard, which allows natural light to flood in. The etched look was accomplished by hand-sanding the surface—a labor-intensive process but much less expensive than buying etched glass.

LEFT The bedroom side of the translucent wall is cleverly composed to offer a tiny built-in bedside table. Every inch of extra space has been used for storage. Surrounding the bed alcove are cubbies for clothes, shoes, and a few hanging items.

Southern Comfort

A QUESTION I HEARD OFTEN AFTER
The Not So Big House came out was, "Can I build a traditional-style
house with a Not So Big floor plan?" The answer is an unequivo-
cal yes. Not So Big concepts can be interpreted in any style. And
to prove it, here are examples from Habersham and Newpoint,
two planned communities near Beaufort, South Carolina, with
details based on the best of the past but
with updated floor plans for the way we
live today.

Eric Moser, who has designed many of
the houses for these two New Urbanist
developments, loved the look of the traditional houses of the past even as a boy,
but he always wondered how people
could live in them. They didn't seem to fit
their residents' lifestyles, with all the
socializing taking place in the kitchen while the formal front
rooms sat vacant. In true Not So Big style, two of Moser's design
hallmarks are making the kitchen the heart of the home and
eliminating the unused formal spaces in order to make money
available for special details.

*The main floor layout is
hardly what you'd expect
to find in a house with
such a traditional exterior.*

ABOVE Many people are captivated by
the look of older homes, with their
simple gabled roofs and gracious front
porches, but their interiors are often ill-
suited to present-day lifestyles. A growing number of planned communities
around the country, like Habersham in
Beaufort, South Carolina, are filling the
void, with exteriors that hark back to
an earlier time and interiors designed
for today.

OPPOSITE The wraparound porch is a
wonderful extension of living space
that's relatively inexpensive to build. It
has the added advantage of making the
house appear significantly larger than it
really is.

Upper Floor

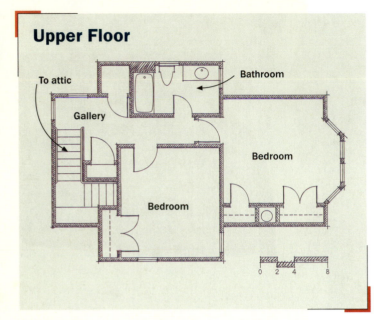

To attic

Gallery

Bathroom

Bedroom

Bedroom

0 2 4 8

If you look at the plan for this home, which was built first in Newpoint and then in Habersham (the house interior shown here), you'll see that the kitchen is centrally located and open to both dining and living areas. An away room opens off the front entry and looks into the living room through double doors. It's hardly the kind of main-floor layout you'd expect to find in a house with such a traditional exterior. But as Eric points out, "Just because you're manipulating the interior spaces doesn't mean you have to give up all the character of these traditional homes."

Modifying an Old Plan

Eric broke with the pattern of the standard floor plan, where each activity has a defined room, usually rectangular or square, and where doors or archways connect one room to the next. By removing the walls between spaces—especially those between the kitchen, living room, and dining area—and by adding wide openings to create long, diagonal views, he made the design work for today's more informal lifestyles. In general, when a space can be seen, it is used. When it can't be seen, it sits dormant.

Main Floor

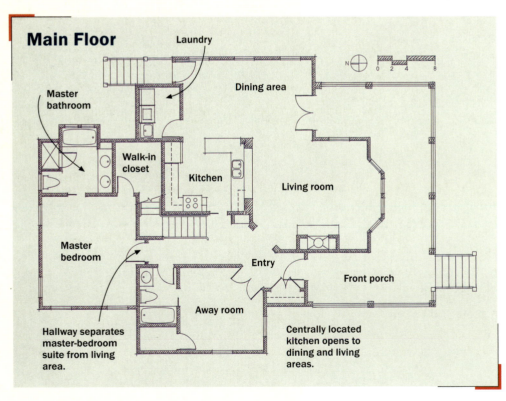

Laundry

Master bathroom

Dining area

Walk-in closet

Kitchen

Living room

Master bedroom

Entry

N 0 2 4 8

Front porch

Away room

Hallway separates master-bedroom suite from living area.

Centrally located kitchen opens to dining and living areas.

Designer:
Moser Design Group, Inc.

Builder:
Southern Traditional
Custom Homes

Size: 2,100 sq. ft.

Location:
Beaufort, S.C.

A hundred years ago, the owners of a house would no more socialize in the kitchen than we would today in our laundry rooms. It was a workspace, the realm of the wife and (if she was lucky) the servants. The kitchen didn't need to have views to other spaces—in fact, it was specifically designed *not* to be seen. But today our lives revolve around the kitchen, and this is where we congregate. If we can't see any other living spaces from here, we tend to crowd into this utilitarian room, while the rest of the house—where we've spent most of our decorating budget—sits unused.

Details Make the Difference

So what gives this updated southern belle her traditional character? It's all in the scale and style of the details. Look at the two columns that mark the entrance from the entry to the living room, for example (see the top photo on p. 174).

They're 14 in. square, much larger than required structurally. But their width makes room for some classic panel detailing that is evocative of a much older home. The crown moldings, door and window casings, and baseboards are also much larger than is typical in a new house today. Certainly these special features add dollars per square foot, but when compared to the savings generated by the elimination of entire rooms, the cost is minor. This was not an expensive home to build, and every-

ABOVE The kitchen is centrally located and opens to both the dining and living areas. The raised countertop serves to hide a messy work surface, but there's no visual separation between cook and company either during meal preparation or cleanup.

LEFT This home's interior detailing is characteristic of its 100-year-old relatives, but the plan is based on Not So Big principles. The away room, visible through the double doors, is close to the front door and can be used as a quiet retreat space, an in-home office, a guest bedroom, or a combination of all three.

where money has been used wisely, making an otherwise standard set of parts into an expression of old-world charm.

Imagine this same interior without these special details. The two columns could have been 4 in. square and sheathed with drywall. The ceilings could have been spray-textured, with no crown moldings to mark the division between walls and ceiling. The openings into the kitchen could have been walled over. And the result? A standard, unadorned developer house.

It really doesn't take a lot to give a house some character, but someone *does* have to design for it, draw it into the blueprints, and make sure it gets built properly. If detailing like this is done sloppily, it can look worse than if it weren't there at all. Although it's important to spend a budget sensibly, this doesn't always mean that you should necessarily select the low bidder. Craftsmanship counts when it comes to building Not So Big, and though it will cost more, it's an investment you'll rejoice in every day.

Furnishing for Comfort

A real challenge when building a period-style home with the kind of floor plan and detailing illustrated here is to resist the urge to decorate with chairs and sofas from that same era. There's only one thing that can sabotage the livability of a Not So Big House, and that's not so comfortable furniture. Fill a room with furnishings designed for looks but not human bodies, and you'll still find yourself leaning on the counter in the kitchen.

This can be a real dilemma for people who've inherited heirloom pieces or spent a

ABOVE Columns like these are a rarity in new homes today and are generally considered a possibility only in a very expensive home. But when the square footage is kept to a reasonable minimum, there's money available for the kinds of special features that add a timeless quality to an otherwise simple structure.

RIGHT The master-bedroom suite is on the main level but separated by a hallway from the everyday living spaces, giving it plenty of acoustical privacy. The stairway's painted risers and natural treads, with three spindles per tread, give it a classic look.

New Urbanism and Traditional Neighborhood Design

*F*or the last few decades, housing developments have focused on expedient construction and automotive convenience rather than on the resulting quality of the neighborhood and community. Trees are stripped from the site, houses are isolated from one another as lots get bigger, and you need a car just to go to the corner store. Front porches have disappeared because there's no pedestrian activity on the streets to watch or share with neighbors, and even the picket fence has been regulated out of existence by well-meaning but misguided development covenants.

Given this state of affairs, it's hardly surprising that there's a nostalgia for a simpler time, when neighbors looked out for one another, lots had mature trees, and streets were just wide enough for two cars to pass.

A movement is taking place across the country to rehumanize the process of residential development. It's known both as New Urbanism and Traditional Neighborhood Design (TND). This concept may be familiar to readers who saw the movie *The Truman Show*, which was filmed at Seaside, Florida, one of the first and best-known new urban communities.

Just as with the Not So Big House, TND emphasizes quality over quantity. Streets have sidewalks, lots are smaller, and the focus on community is brought back by preserving existing landscape features (especially large trees), building front porches, and using carefully proportioned and well-crafted details. Newpoint has been in existence for only six years, but it looks as though it's been around for centuries. And Habersham, which was

started just two years ago, promises to have this same timeless quality. In our search for home, there's a lot we can learn from the TND movement.

lot of money in the past on furniture for a large, formal house. One strategy is to locate prize pieces in an out-of-the-way corner where they can be admired without monopolizing a primary living space, as has been done here with the very pretty but not particularly inviting wooden love seat next to the French door (see the photo on p. 176). Meanwhile the furniture in the living room has an overstuffed comfort that, though not something you'd find in an antiques magazine, invites you to stretch out and settle in. It's an unfortunate reality that much of what we consider stylish today inhibits the very living we long to do in our homes.

There's only one thing that can sabotage the livability of a Not So Big House, and that's not so comfortable furniture.

ABOVE Ceilings throughout the main level are 9 ft. tall, and moldings are ornate and substantial, in keeping with the proportions of an older home. But instead of traditional rooms, here spaces flow from one to the next without doors and dividing walls to define them—a more contemporary approach to interior design.

A Change of Face

Another lesson that can be learned from this house is just how different an exterior can look with variations in its detailing. This same basic house has been built several times in the communities of Habersham and Newpoint. Though the plans are essentially identical, the finishing details are quite different.

Looking at the front elevations of two of the homes, you can see that both have a wraparound porch on the main level that looks both gracious and welcoming. But the version built in Newpoint (top right) has significantly more gingerbread decorating its surfaces. It also has a steeper pitch to the main roof and an additional balcony on the second floor. The closely spaced porch columns with their connecting brackets make this house seem more introverted than its less-decorated sister. It feels more private, as though in stepping onto this porch you move behind a veil. By contrast, the Habersham house (bottom right) has a more open demeanor.

It's not uncommon for people to reject a plan because they don't like the house "face," when in fact this is very easily altered. Just like the interior, it's the details—the slope of the roof, the special moldings, the width of the trimwork, and the proportions of each element in relation to one another—that give a house much of its character. When arranged with an eye for composition, learning from the past but designing for today, the options for variety and personal expression are almost infinite.

Although I don't advocate a retreat into the past, there's much we have forgotten about how to make a house look and feel like home. We can learn by looking and listening to our senses and, in so doing, rediscover those things we miss while eliminating those that no longer work today. Communities like Newpoint and Habersham, and houses like this one, are a major step in that direction.

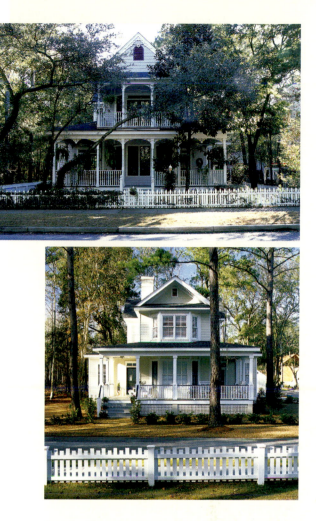

ABOVE These two houses have the same house plan as the house featured in this chapter but with different clothing. What makes them appear so different is the detailing. If you count the columns on the porches of both houses, for example, you'll see that the one in Newpoint (top) has a different visual rhythm from its sister in Habersham (bottom). The location of the steps up to the wraparound porch in Habersham invites you into this house, while their central positioning in Newpoint, surprisingly, makes the entrance a more private affair. This is because when you arrive at the former you are aligned with the front door, while the latter delivers you to a living-room window.

An Accessible House for One

OPPOSITE The bathroom has been designed with plenty of room for a wheelchair to turn around, but the room doesn't have an institutional feel. The goal throughout the house was to integrate accessible design features in an unobtrusive way.

LEFT Designed as a quiet retreat with a Not So Big budget, this cabin quickly became a year-round home. The construction materials are off the shelf and inexpensive—4x8 sheets of Hardipanel, concrete blocks, and standard asphalt shingles—but artful design makes the whole more than the sum of its parts.

W HEN YOU'RE DESIGNING A NOT SO Big House, it's important to think not only about your present lifestyle but also about your future needs. For example, a far-sighted couple designing a house for their young family might want to allow for a future bedroom on the main level for when they are older. The reality is that we all age, and if we build for a lifetime, we have to keep future needs in mind.

In recent years, there's been much written about universal design, inclusive design, and life-span design. These are all names for the same intent: to design products and environments for the widest possible variety of people. Although in public buildings it's important to make such accommodations from the outset, in residences, design solutions can be more specific to the individual's personal needs and can be modified over time as those needs become clear. The difficulty comes in determining

By designing an open plan and building in only the most crucial elements from the beginning, you can create a house that will be easy to remodel as needs change.

just how much to build in from the start and how much to leave for remodeling when the day comes.

Sometimes life throws us an unexpected curve ball, and there's no way of anticipating what needs we'll have even a year or two down the road. This was the case for the owner of the home shown here. She had been diagnosed with multiple sclerosis, and her doctor suggested that she could benefit from having a stress-free environment in a natural setting to get away to now and then.

The owner approached architect Geoff Prentiss, who found her a secluded piece of property on Orcas Island surrounded by marsh and trees, which perfectly met her needs. The house he designed for her there, which started out as a place of retreat to be used primarily for day trips from her home in Seattle, is very simple: a long gabled structure with just one main room, a bathroom, and a closet.

What was originally intended for daytime use quickly became a year-round home, as the owner discovered the restorative quality of the site. Although the amenities are minimal and the plan is rendered down to its simplest components, it serves her needs and feeds her spirit. It is an excellent demonstration of the fact that for many of us, it's the quality of a place, far more than the specifics of a floor plan, that makes a house a home.

Main Floor

Bathroom is big enough to allow wheelchair to turn around.

All entrances are double French doors to allow wheelchair access.

Deck

Kitchen

Window seat doubles as bed by night.

Dining table doubles as kitchen work surface.

Living room

Closet

Bookshelves

Storage

Deck

N 0 2 4 8

Architect:
Prentiss Architects, Inc.
Builder:
Ravenhill Construction
Size: 1,215 sq. ft.
Location:
Orcas Island, Wash.

Getting Around

Although the owner was fully mobile during the design process, she needed to plan for an uncertain future, which included the strong possibility of her eventually needing a wheelchair to get around. She didn't want the house to look like it was built for a wheelchair, however, and Geoff made that a primary design objective. As a result, you'd never guess that this house was designed for someone with impaired mobility.

One of the most difficult issues to address when it comes to accessibility is how much to anticipate in the design process. For some, the most functional solution once the wheelchair is a full-time necessity may not be aesthetically or practically acceptable until then. By designing an open plan and building in only the most crucial elements from the beginning, you can create a house that will be easy to remodel as needs change.

This is an important consideration for those who want to design their homes to allow for the possibility of future mobility issues. It's possible to spend a lot of money on universal-design features that may not ultimately be useful, while other unanticipated features become a must. My suggestion to clients contemplating this issue is to make the walls and doors work for wheelchair accessibility, and accept that if mobility becomes an issue, some remodeling

ABOVE For accessibility, the house is primarily one large room with an attached bathroom and closet. Four sets of French doors open wide to connect inside with out. Kitchen, dining, and living areas are all housed under the long gable roof.

It's the quality of a place, far more than the specifics of a floor plan, that makes a house a home.

will be needed. You can then tailor that remodeling to suit the particular disability rather than a generic standard.

This is the strategy that Geoff employed. All the entrances into the house are double French doors, specially designed to be opened with one hand. The extra width allows for a wheelchair to move through with ease, without the oversized look that comes with extrawide single doors.

The kitchen counters are not open below, as they typically would be in universal design, but they are only 32 in. high, 4 in. lower than a standard countertop. This height allows comfortable access from either a standing or a sitting position. The dining table, which is of course open below, also doubles as a kitchen work surface. And the bathroom is designed with plenty of room for a wheelchair to circulate, complete with lipless shower and strategically located grab bars.

ABOVE The dining-room table doubles as a kitchen work surface and, as in an old farmhouse kitchen, is flexible enough to accommodate all sorts of tasks, from eating to creating art projects to paying bills. The kitchen counter itself is set 4 in. lower than normal to allow easy access for the owner, who may someday be dependent upon a wheelchair to get around.

RIGHT Doorways are wide, and the shower stall has no lip to trip over or roll over in a wheelchair. Although this makes the shower a little less convenient for someone without impaired mobility, if a wheelchair is a likely eventuality, there'll be no major remodeling required when it happens.

OPPOSITE The birch plywood ceiling gives a golden glow to the light as it bounces around this room. When that effect is combined with the many windows, contrasting walls, and radiant concrete floor, the room has a warmth to it, despite the hardness of the surfaces. In the Pacific Northwest, making the most of the diffuse daylight is crucial, since sunny days are rare in the winter and spring.

Alcoves Make the Room

In many ways, this small house is like one spacious great room. But there are some apparently insignificant details that make it far more livable than most such rooms. If you look at the floor plan, you'll see that the main rectangle of the room has a number of small alcoves added, which house window seats, bookshelves, and places for freestanding furniture.

Now, if you look at the photos of the space, you can see that the ceiling is brought down over these areas, defining each as its own space and creating shelter around each activity, a fundamental strategy in making Not So Big work. It's such a simple gesture, yet without it the room would feel very different.

OPPOSITE **Beneath the window seats that flank the fireplace, open shelves store everything from blankets to books to briefcases. The vertical dividers between shelves are finished with madrona branches from the neighboring woods. Introducing a natural element from the site lends a spirit and uniqueness often missing in contemporary homes.**

BELOW **The main room has some subtleties of design that make it work better for everyday living than the typical great room. Along both side walls, small alcoves create places for a variety of activities and functions, like this small library nook.**

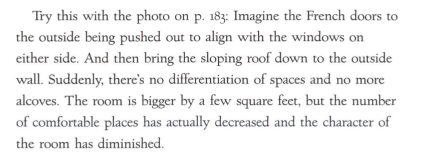

Try this with the photo on p. 183: Imagine the French doors to the outside being pushed out to align with the windows on either side. And then bring the sloping roof down to the outside wall. Suddenly, there's no differentiation of spaces and no more alcoves. The room is bigger by a few square feet, but the number of comfortable places has actually decreased and the character of the room has diminished.

Window Patterns

Another strength of the room is its connection to the outdoors. Geoff refers to windows as the eyes of the house. Though the budget was tight and most of the materials used are very economical, the windows are custom-made. Each one has horizontal mullions that align with those of adjacent windows, giving the room a distinct rhythm and a personality all its own.

The tall windows flanking the fireplace serve an important role. First, they bring the room into proportion. Had these windows been the same size as their neighbors, the end wall of the house would have seemed top heavy and the room less humanly scaled and less comfortable. Place your thumb over the upper window in the photo on p. 183 to see what I mean.

But also these windows almost look like eyes. Remember how, as a child, you'd see faces in the forms of clouds,

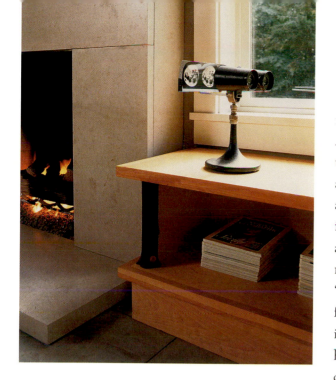

rocks, and tree branches? As adults we still have this reflex, but most of us are not as consciously aware of it. Still, it has an influence on how we feel about a place. A house or room with a friendly "face" tends to make us feel more warmly toward it. One without such a harmonious composition can make us feel uncomfortable, without our knowing why. This effect, which we recognize easily in a two-dimensional surface like a painting, is just as important—if not as apparent—when you are working in a three-dimensional space.

A great lesson of this house is that when we design a place that we think of as a cabin retreat rather than a year-round house, we allow ourselves to accommodate our needs in innovative ways. The results typically require less space and often fit our real lifestyle better than a conventional house. This spirit of innovation gets to the heart of building Not So Big. For those trying to plan for a less mobile future, the attitudes embodied in this house are based on practicality, but they are life affirming rather than life diminishing. If we surround ourselves with images of the depletion that's ahead of us, we're likely to reflect that attitude in how we live. But if we surround ourselves with the warmth of forms and colors we love, we are likely to live much more fully. By building Not So Big, there's money available to add some special features to accommodate mobility needs and still make a home that's beautiful and filled with places of inspiration.

Double-Duty Window Seats

Where do you sleep in a house without bedrooms? If you're living alone, wherever you like. The owner of this house had originally planned to buy a sleigh bed, but she liked the window seats so much that she decided to use one as her bed at night. Just a pane of glass away from the outdoors, it's more like a sleeping porch than an interior room.

As in a Japanese house, where futons are rolled out for sleeping and put away during the day, the room changes use from day to night, rather than requiring the owner to move to a different part of the house. This can work well for one person, although it may be less acceptable for couples or families. Still, it illustrates how a single space can be made to do double duty in unconventional ways that are particularly suited to the occupant's preferences. Just because something is unusual doesn't mean you shouldn't do it.

A Place of Cool Remove

BUILDING NOT SO BIG IS ALL ABOUT making choices that will enhance your life, and sometimes those choices involve more than a floor plan. For David and Ellen, the choice was between the flat, urban landscape of Houston, where their lives were focused around work, and a quiet retreat in the country, with a slower pace that was more in keeping with their joys and values. David and Ellen had lived in the Houston suburbs for many years, but after visiting friends in the hill country outside Austin, they realized they were ready for a change of scenery. Only a few weeks later they had purchased some acreage, hired architect Sharon Tyler Hoover, and started to plan their new house.

When selecting a site for a Not So Big House, it's important to locate it so that land and house blend seamlessly, as though the house grew from the land.

ABOVE **French doors open wide on either side of the house to two symmetrical porches, one screened, the other open. The supporting posts and pilasters are scaled to the rest of the house, though they are larger than actually required to support the metal roof. Visual proportion can be as important as bearing capacity.**

Finding the Right Spot

The property had a number of potential building sites at the top of a hill, with spectacular views on all sides. But David and Ellen didn't feel that the house would look appropriate up there, visible from miles around, and David, who'd been used to flat land all his life, felt vulnerable in these high spots. As it turned out, their instinctive reactions to the site were sound. The highest point may look impressive at first glance, but building there tends to separate the house from, rather than integrate it with, its surroundings.

When selecting a site for a Not So Big House, it's important to locate it so that land and house blend seamlessly, as though the house grew from the land and resides there as naturally as the neighboring vegetation. David and Ellen decided to find just the right location by camping in different spots along the hillside, in order to get a feel for each potential site. They discovered that they preferred the land closer to the creek at the bottom of the hill and settled on an area not far from the swimming hole—a feature they knew they'd use every day.

Night Breezes

Sharon was pleased with their site selection, not only because it allowed for easy integration with the land but also because it offered an excellent opportunity to take advantage of the naturally occurring wind patterns and rising and falling air currents. As the land cools at night, air sinks and flows downstream, much like a river, collecting in the low pockets. Setting the house lower on the hill let her take advantage of that effect to help cool the house naturally.

Cool Comfort

Although we typically think of comfort in terms of cozy alcoves and light-filled living spaces, on a practical level, creating comfort also encompasses issues of heating and cooling. Most parts of the United States have to contend with varying degrees of summer heat and winter cold, but in David and Ellen's location, even the winter months are warm. It's a little-discussed fact that houses in hot climates expend as much energy for cooling as their more northerly neighbors do for heating. But a house in a hot climate requires very different strategies to keep it comfortable, and designing a house that will largely cool itself is quite an art.

Finding a professional who really understands how to take advantage of your site and climate to minimize long-term energy consumption can save a lot of money and resources over the lifetime of the house. The design the architect developed for this home is based on her knowledge of the climate of the area, and it is clearly very different from a design appropriate for a more northerly location.

This was especially important to David and Ellen, who wanted to let the outside in as much as possible. With all the windows closed tight and the air-conditioning running, there's a sense of isolation from the vitality of the surrounding landscape. In keeping with their desire for a simpler, less hurried way of life, they wanted their home to let nature's calming influence inside whenever possible.

So Sharon took the natural airflow of the site as a primary inspiration for the house, creating high awning windows to catch the falling night air and stone interior walls to retain some of the coolness for daytime use. By sliding the house in between some of the tall elms on the site and creating a cascade of roofs with wide overhangs above porches, decks, and windows, the interior is kept comfortable with only minimal need for air-conditioning.

Although we typically think of comfort in terms of cozy alcoves and light-filled living spaces, on a practical level, creating comfort also encompasses issues of heating and cooling.

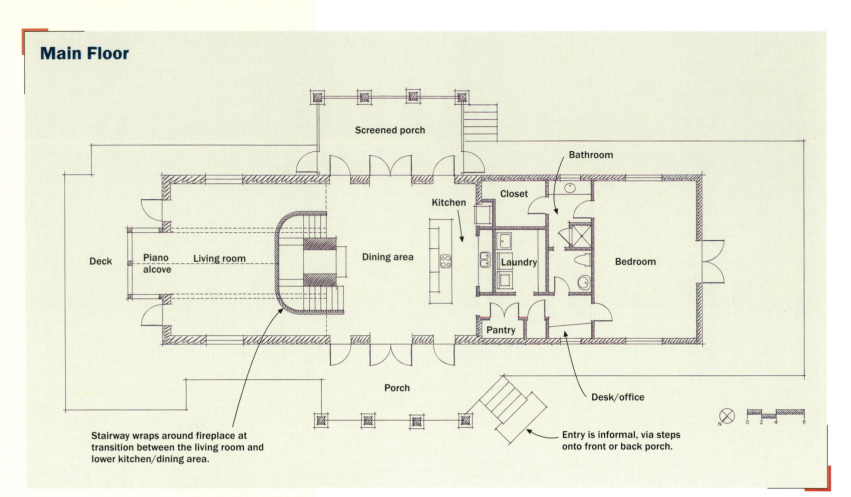

Screened porch

Bathroom

Closet

Kitchen

Deck

Piano alcove   Living room

Dining area

Laundry

Bedroom

Pantry

Desk/office

Porch

N   0 2 4   8

Stairway wraps around fireplace at transition between the living room and lower kitchen/dining area.

Entry is informal, via steps onto front or back porch.

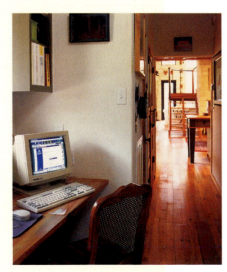

RIGHT Just down the hallway from the kitchen, Ellen's desk alcove is tucked between the pantry and the guest bedroom suite (which will evolve into the master suite when climbing stairs becomes a challenge). From here she can keep an eye on what's happening in the kitchen but still be in a quiet pocket of space away from the rest of the house.

Build What You'll Use

You enter this house very informally—in fact, there's no designated front entry at all. When you live out in the country, there's no street to face and no one you need to impress with a grand entry. Those who come to the house are almost always family or friends; for those rare occasions when a stranger arrives, the stairs up onto the porch from the driveway provide adequate invitation. This is a good example of how easy it is to design functions into our homes that are superfluous for our particular situation. It may seem odd not to have a front entry, but if it's never likely to be used, why have one?

Upper Floor

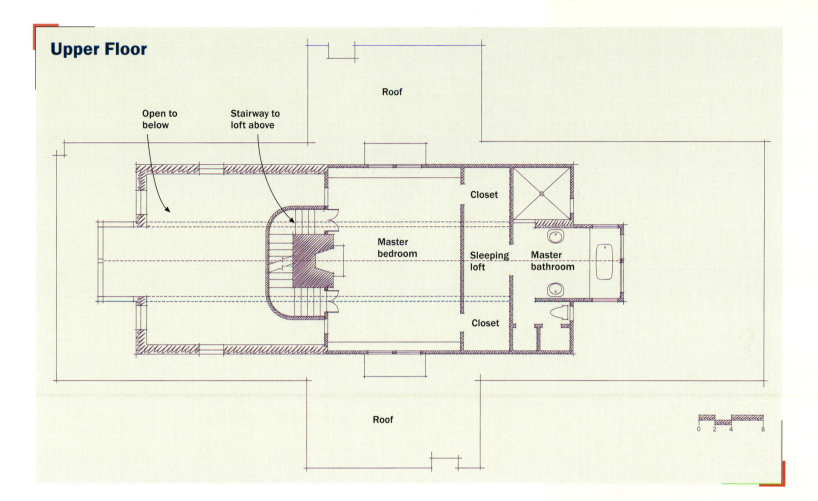

Open to below

Stairway to loft above

Roof

Closet

Master bedroom

Sleeping loft

Master bathroom

Closet

Roof

0 2 4 8

This same kind of thinking applies to formal living rooms and dining rooms. These rooms typically get built because we're led to believe that a "normal" house is supposed to have them. But if you won't use these formal rooms, don't build them. It doesn't make sense to spend thousands of dollars on a room that gets used only once or twice a year. One alternative is to do what David and Ellen have done: They have guests over frequently, but rather than build a separate formal dining room and living room, they've made rooms that serve them well on a daily basis but are also excellent for entertaining.

Architect:
Sharon Tyler Hoover, Architect

Builder:
David Staland

Size: 2,400 sq. ft.

Location:
Wimberley, Tex.

A Study in Contrasts

The interior of this home is a weaving of contrasting qualities: light and dark, bright and subdued, solid and void, tall and short. Contrast is a rarely used design tool in most new homes today, but when employed successfully, it can have a powerful effect. For example, many people say they want a house with lots of windows. But if you make a house that has too many windows, they lose their appeal and the house becomes a place that's too exposed for everyday living. There's no place of shelter—no contrast.

In this home, the windowed walls of the piano alcove are set adjacent to solid planes of stone—the exact opposite of the openness and transparency of the glass. The tall living room contrasts with the kitchen and dining area, which has a much darker, more introverted character. With 9-ft. ceilings, this space is low and sheltered compared to the height and airiness of the living room. If the entire main level had only the qualities of either space, it would seem monotonous. It's the presence of opposites that makes each area inviting. It's the same with the small splashes of color introduced by the tile mosaic in the kitchen and bathrooms—the bright colors draw attention to the subtlety of the rest of the color scheme.

ABOVE The dining area is screened from the kitchen by an island that doubles as a china cabinet and desk. The table's rustic character makes it ideal for both everyday use and formal meals. The kitchen itself is built into the stone wall and to the casual observer seems more like a work of art than a workplace. (PHOTO COURTESY HESTER AND HARDAWAY PHOTOGRAPHERS.)

RIGHT On the work side of the kitchen island, the cooktop is sheltered behind the china cabinet. The broken-tile motif, a reflection of the area's Hispanic influence, provides a colorful counterpoint to the more subdued coloring of the natural stone and wood.

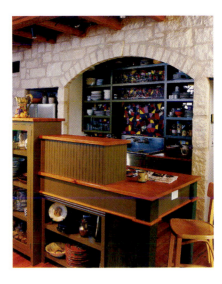

ABOVE The detailing of the island is intended to make it look like an old kitchen table, with pine plank surface and thick painted legs.

RIGHT This is a house full of contrasts. The living room, used for frequent entertaining, is tall and light filled, in contrast to the lower, more introverted kitchen and dining area.

A Home with Soul

Sharon is a strong advocate of natural and recycled materials, and she used them here to good effect, giving the house an informality and warmth more typical of an older structure that's gained character with the passing years. The kitchen and dining area, with its recycled pine flooring and countertops and the exposed joist ceiling, has some of the timeworn qualities of an old barn. It's comfortable and welcoming, and the kitchen is so well integrated into the decor of the dining area that it hardly looks like a kitchen at all. By using materials such as stone and wood, with the markings of years of wear and tear, the house gains a depth and meaning that almost everyone who visits feels and comments on.

Since they relocated to the hill country, David and Ellen have been surprised to discover how many friends are willing to make the trek from the city to visit them, and they're fairly certain that the house itself is a big part of the attraction. There's a spirit of welcome here and a timelessness that transports anyone who enters to a place where the important things in life are not written down in a Daytimer organizer or PalmPilot. For David and Ellen, this is just what they were looking for. Now they call it home.

LEFT There's no reason that all the fixtures in a bathroom have to be at the same height. Here, a claw-foot tub has been raised to take advantage of the views.

OPPOSITE The staircase winds around the central chimney, making the fireplace into a cozy alcove under the landing. The views through to the dining area and kitchen on either side are wide and inviting, creating a strong connection between the introverted and extroverted sides of the house.

Up Close

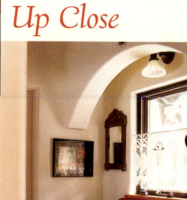

The built-ins in this home look more like pieces of furniture than standard cabinetry. This bathroom vanity resembles an old-style washstand, except of course for the modern sink and faucet. This is really no more difficult to accomplish than building standard cabinetry, and the effect is evocative of a much older home.

Elegant Simplicity

T̲HE SUMMER HOME DESIGNED BY architect Jim Estes for a retired couple in Jamestown, Rhode Island, is a study in simplicity. Created with an unerring eye for proportion and a careful execution of classic details, this house captivates anyone who enters it. It gracefully illustrates how beauty can be the result of economy of means and how a plan does not have to be complex to have impact.

When Marion and Bill originally approached their architect, they were envisioning a much larger house—a place with plenty of room for visiting children and grandchildren. But after the first round of design work with Jim, they realized that what they really wanted was a place with a more intimate scale—a place that the two of them could enjoy together. A large, rambling house can be great for family reunions, but it's often overwhelming for day-to-day living. Here, visitors would be welcomed, but they would not be made the focus of the design.

There's nothing flamboyant about this house, yet it is masterful in its understated presence.

It is often the simplicity of a plan that gives the resulting home its charm. The key is in the third dimension.

Whether to size a house for yourself or for your extended family is a common dilemma. In an effort to accommodate everyone, houses can get very large, when in fact the people who live there every day need very little space to feel at home. Jim solved the problem by designing an open floor plan with a main living area that can serve comfortably for a couple or a crowd. This allows the house to be considerably smaller yet actually work better for both purposes.

Main Floor

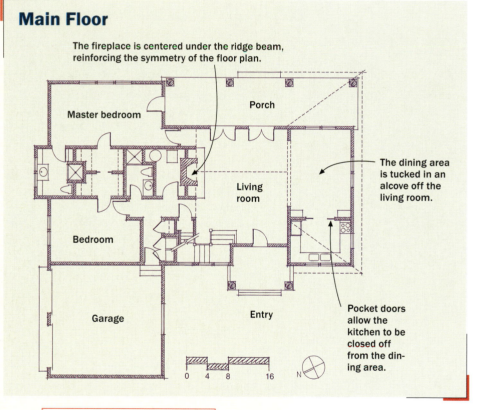

The fireplace is centered under the ridge beam, reinforcing the symmetry of the floor plan.

Master bedroom

Porch

The dining area is tucked in an alcove off the living room.

Living room

Bedroom

Garage

Entry

Pocket doors allow the kitchen to be closed off from the dining area.

0 4 8 16

N

Architect:
Estes/Twombly Architects, Inc.
Builder: Allan Randall, Construction
Size: 1,800 sq. ft.
Location: Jamestown, R.I.

A Simple Plan

Marion and Bill wanted the house to fit unobtrusively into its neighborhood, a 19th-century Quaker summer colony near Jamestown. Many of the homes have strong, simple forms, with symmetrical exteriors and wide porches facing the water. Jim suggested a straightforward plan based on what he calls "bilateral symmetry." This means that the house is organized around a central axis, which in this case bisects the fireplace. The floor plan is essentially symmetrical on either side of this axis, with segments of space carved out under the broad sheltering roof.

RIGHT Although this room has a high cathedral ceiling, it is not overwhelming when only one or two people are using it, as so many great rooms are today. The exposed rafters and the pattern of woodwork above the fireplace break up the scale of the room and add a texture reminiscent of houses of the past.

ABOVE The kitchen is small, with pocket doors that allow it to be completely separated from the dining area on formal occasions and open when only family or friends are present. As might be expected, the doors are almost always open.

Many homeowners want a plan with more complexity, which automatically adds to the cost, since every angle and curve has construction ramifications. Marion and Bill were unusual in accepting a plan that, on paper at least, looked undistinguished. But as Jim admirably demonstrates, it is often the simplicity of a plan that gives the resulting home its charm. The key is in the third dimension.

The living room is at the heart of this plan and acts as a focus for activity, with dining area and stairway alcoves opening onto it. With its high ceiling, the room could easily have become sterile and overwhelming. But here—with the ridge centered above the fireplace, the beams and rafters exposed, and the height variations introduced in the alcoves—the result is an ample gathering space for friends and family that's just as comfortable for two.

Say It with Contrast

A mistake often made in houses today is that every ceiling is the same height, leaving no way to differentiate between spaces. This house works because of the contrasts, both in ceiling height and in the exposed structure. Take away the beams and rafters, and make the dining area the same height as the rest of the living room, and you have your typical, palatially proportioned drywalled barn—hardly the place you'd want to curl up with a good book. It doesn't take a lot to bring a space down to human scale. In this house, the shape and size of the dining area help do the trick. The roof here runs perpendicular to the main roof, which helps give the vaulting heights of the living room a more manageable and intelligible dimension. It's almost as if this sloped ceiling slows down the space, and brings it to a gentle halt. This is mirrored on a smaller scale in the kitchen ceiling, which opens off the dining area.

A mistake often made in houses today is that every ceiling is the same height, leaving no way to differentiate between spaces.

LEFT There is a clear hierarchy of activity areas in this house, and their importance is defined by the ceiling height. The dining area is attached to the living room like a lean-to, with its ceiling descending to only 7 ft. at the far windows. The room becomes an inviting alcove off the living room, subordinate in both floor area and ceiling height.

Up Close

Shutters on most modern houses are merely decorative, but on this house they really work and

are closed in the winter months, when the house is largely unused. Because they are sized to fit the windows, the proportions look right.

The textural quality created by the beams and rafters is also important in creating a comfortable scale. In conventional stud-frame construction, we cover the rafters and fill the space with insulation. Here, Jim put the insulation above the rafters and roof sheathing, to get the look and feel of an old summer cottage. When our eye receives visual information that allows us to interpret scale, we often feel more secure. Subconsciously, we know how much distance there is between one rafter and the next. We see the pattern of shadow and light made by the sequence of rafters. And together these visual cues add up to a place that feels like home.

Grandmother's House

Many Not So Big Houses draw their inspiration from houses of the past. An archetypal image of home that we carry in our minds is what I like to call "grandmother's house," an assemblage of images composed of memories from childhood—perhaps a special window seat in the kitchen, a cozy fireplace, or a wonderful porch swing. Parts of this composite home may also be drawn from images we remember from cherished childhood fairy tales and paintings, like Carl Larsson's images of idyllic Scandinavian home life.

It's often the easy comfort of a grandmother's house that encourages children and grandchildren to visit; the closer a house is to the archetype, the more at home they feel and the more they want to return. The simple home shown here embodies many of the necessary characteristics, including generous porches, window shutters, exposed rafters, and a classic cottage form. It's very helpful to keep this archetype in mind when you're planning a Not So Big House, which is by its nature a smaller, cozier home.

This gracious porch, sheltered by a wide overhanging roof, is a perfect width for enjoying the natural surroundings—even when it's raining. Any wider and the proportions wouldn't feel right for the house.

Getting It Right

Because the house was designed primarily for summer living, the porch was a key area. The main living spaces open onto it, and the long views through the house to the porch beckon you to sit quietly and gaze at the water. At 8 ft. wide, the porch is the perfect size for sitting. Make it much wider, and you start to feel too far away from the surrounding landscape. Make it much narrower, and it's difficult for people to get by.

During the winter months, when the house is largely unused, the heat is turned down to around 40°F and the window shutters are closed for the season. Shutters today are typically used as a decorative motif, but we forget that they used to serve a real function—and, as in this house, sometimes still do. One of the most satisfying aspects of the exterior of this house is the size of the shutters. They really do cover the windows when they're closed. So when they're open, they look right. We instinctively respond to good proportions, even if we don't always know why.

All told, there's nothing flamboyant about this house, yet it is masterful in its understated presence. Beauty arises not from cleverness so much as from care, from taking time to scale each element appropriately in relation to the next, and from paring down to the essentials: simplicity and elegance. It sounds deceptively easy, but the art is in knowing how we respond to space and light. Proportion is key, as this house illustrates so well.

ABOVE The master bedroom is just off the porch, and its alignment takes full advantage of the landscape. Its doorway acts as a wonderful picture frame, setting off the view down the length of the porch and inviting you to come out and enjoy the sunrise. It speaks of peacefulness and relaxation.

LEFT Daylight pours down the staircase and into the living room below. The stair is designed as an alcove of sorts—almost a room in its own right. The upper landing that leads to the guest bedroom creates a hallway with a low ceiling on the floor below. It's largely the contrasts in ceiling height that make this house so appealing.

Upstairs, Downstairs

Within days of the 1991 fire that swept through the Oakland/Berkeley Hills, the phones at the offices of architects Jacobson Silverstein Winslow were ringing off the hook. Though many families chose the more expedient route of finding a builder, selecting a standard house plan, and rebuilding as quickly as possible, others—like Murray Silverstein's clients David and Julia—saw the loss of their old house as an opportunity to design the home of their dreams. A young professional couple without children, they didn't want or need a large house. But they did want whatever they built to be beautiful and tranquil, to provide a respite from the frenetic pace of their busy professional lives.

Living spaces are above and sleeping spaces below, an unconventional configuration in most areas but a common approach in hill country.

David and Julia are fond of the classic Bay Area modernism of the early 20th century, especially that influenced by Japanese architecture, such as the work of architect Bernard Maybeck. They

OPPOSITE The roof is designed to resemble a large tent, protecting the rooms below. Two beams on either side of the ridge run the length of the house. They not only support the roof load but also serve as the primary organizing devices for the spaces below, culminating at the fireplace wall.

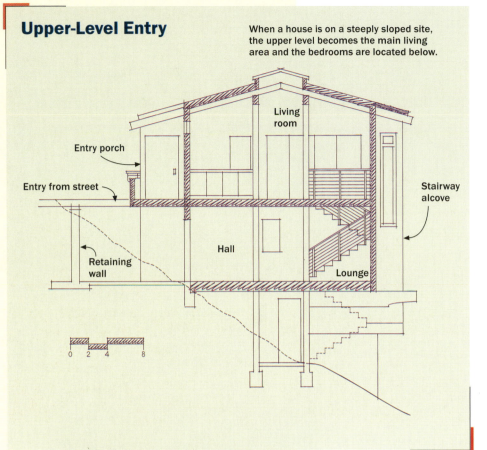

Upper-Level Entry

When a house is on a steeply sloped site, the upper level becomes the main living area and the bedrooms are located below.

Entry porch

Entry from street

Retaining wall

Hall

Living room

Stairway alcove

Lounge

0 2 4 8

particularly like the simplicity of a single, almost tentlike space under a broad sheltering roof, with bump-outs added where needed. Their site, like many in the area of the fire, is steeply sloped, with access from the street onto a main floor that, it turns out, is also the upper level. So it was decided early on that living spaces would be above and sleeping spaces below, an unconventional configuration in most areas but a common approach in hill country.

Zen Corners

The site is located on a creek, with houses dotted fairly densely along both banks. Rather than take the obvious approach of locating windows to look directly across to the opposite bank, Murray reasoned that the house and its views would seem more expansive if all the windows faced either up or down the creek, thus lengthening the visible distance. The strategy works masterfully. This is a house of open, light-filled corners—in fact, almost every room has a corner window. This, combined with the layout of the house, where rooms flow into one another with few interior walls, lets you look along the diagonal, through space after space, and then out to the creek beyond.

These windows, however, aren't typical corner windows. Normally, a corner-window configuration is composed of two windows with a vertical divider, or mullion, at the corner. This mullion transfers the weight of the roof and upper level down

Long diagonal views dramatically increase the perceived size of the house.

through the structure to the foundation. Here, though, there's no vertical post at the corner. The house seems to defy gravity, with the interior space flowing out into the surroundings without obstruction. It is this, more than any other feature, that gives this home its Zen-like serenity. These really aren't corners at all. They're the absence of corners. And the long diagonal views dramatically increase the perceived size of the house.

A Flow-Through House

Many Not So Big Houses have very open plans, and rooms are often identified by changes in ceiling height rather than by walls. This house employs a different strategy, using a pod of space to define the rooms. It's similar to the U-shaped refrigerator wall in the Branford, Connecticut, house (see p. 50), but on a larger scale, using a central object to separate rooms from one another while still allowing the space to flow through—a bit like water swirling around rocks in a stream. In this house, it's the powder room, entry closet, and refrigerator alcove that serve as the rock (see the main floor plan on p. 210). If you were to remove this pod of space, the floor plan would be completely open.

ABOVE There are corner windows in almost every room, letting the view continue unobstructed out into the canyon beyond. At this corner, the room is bumped out to make a window-seat bay, with the side walls providing back rests. Drawers below the window seats provide extra storage.

LEFT On the lower level, a corner window in the bathroom reveals a tiny sunken garden, which is also visible as you enter the house on the level above. When the tub and the windowsill are at almost the same height, bathers can see out of the window. Raise the sill a little, and the view disappears.

OPPOSITE Though the kitchen is tucked away from view of the living room, it is open to the dining area, which serves both formal and informal purposes. Even from the dining table, however, the kitchen prep and cleanup areas are out of sight, cleverly hidden around the corner.

RIGHT Accordion-style French doors allow the entire dining-area wall to disappear and the room to extend out onto the deck beyond. The windows in the kitchen come all the way down to the countertop, further obscuring the distinction between inside and out. (PHOTO COURTESY JACOBSON SILVERSTEIN WINSLOW.)

BELOW Just visible on the right of this photo, you can see the refrigerator, which is part of a pod of space that separates the floor plan into identifiable rooms and hides the kitchen from the front entry and living room.

When you can see everything from everywhere, there's no mystery, no exploration necessary. Some people like this, but many feel that it makes a house less inviting. It's more like an open field and less like a path through the woods, with interesting places to stop and visit along the way. Looking at the photographs of this home, you can feel its intimacy and warmth. This is in large part due to the way it reveals itself gradually, rather than all at once. It invites you to flow with it through the spaces to discover its secrets.

Kitchen Alcove

Many people who like the idea of building Not So Big, with the kitchen, dining, and living areas all open to one another, are concerned that the kitchen (and kitchen messes) will be constantly on view. Here, the kitchen, though open to the dining area, is more enclosed than any of the other spaces on the main floor. It's surrounded on three sides by walls and on the fourth by the powder-room pod. It's not visible from the front entry or from the living room, but it is connected through spatial flow.

There's an art to making the kitchen a partially hidden alcove. It needs to be open enough to the dining area to allow the cook to converse with family members at the table. But for formal occasions, it works best if the messier work surfaces, particularly those around the sink and cooktop, are hidden from view. By tucking the main work areas into an alcove, you have the illusion of complete openness without the less-than-desirable reminder that there's still cleanup to be done.

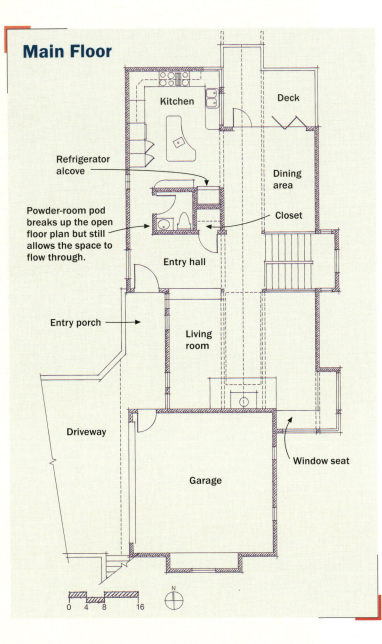

Main Floor

Kitchen

Deck

Refrigerator alcove

Dining area

Powder-room pod breaks up the open floor plan but still allows the space to flow through.

Closet

Entry hall

Entry porch

Living room

Driveway

Window seat

Garage

0   4   8   16

Psychological Breathing Space

Small houses typically won't feel small as long as there's plenty of "psychological breathing space" as you enter and move about the house. A tight hallway, a tiny landing at the top or bottom of a staircase, or an entryway that's too small to greet guests comfortably is a surefire way to make a house feel tiny, even if it's actually quite large. We tend to remember the inconvenience of being crammed into too small a space—just think of a toilet compartment on an airplane and you'll know what I mean. When you're building Not So Big, it's important to make sure that the circulation space—the way that you move from point A to point B—is generous and that stairways are wider than the bare minimum.

David and Julia's house beautifully illustrates how a stairway can become almost a room in itself, opening graciously onto the upper- and lower-level hallways, both of which are bigger than might be expected for a house of this size. The landings, stairway, and skylit window alcove provide essential psychological breathing space. Together, they become a focal point of the house that's visible from many areas, emphasizing the connection between the upper and lower levels and inviting you to come and explore the rest of the house.

The Not So Big Laundry

Laundry requirements vary dramatically from family to family. For a couple without kids, a small closet may be sufficient, as long as there's enough space for folding. In this house, the laundry is within easy reach of the master bedroom, where most of the wash is generated, and when not in use, it disappears. In all, the laundry occupies just 16 sq. ft.

If a compact laundry center will work for you, consider a stackable washer/dryer unit and locate it off a space that can readily do double duty on laundry day. A full-size stackable unit is an excellent space saver, making room for adjacent cabinets. If you use a standard side-by-side top-loading washer and dryer, the top surfaces are inconvenient to use as counter space. And the popular European front-loading machines, though elegant, prevent you from adding any items once the washing cycle has begun—an issue for some.

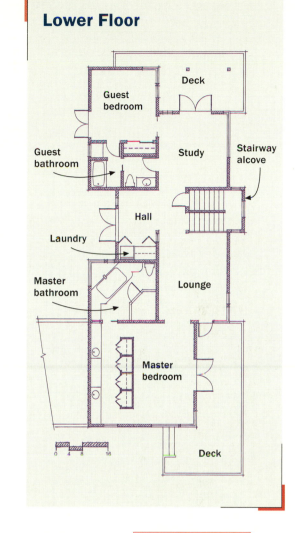

Lower Floor

Deck

Guest bedroom

Study

Stairway alcove

Guest bathroom

Hall

Laundry

Lounge

Master bathroom

Master bedroom

0 4 8 16

Deck

Architect:
Jacobson Silverstein
Winslow Architects

Builder:
Winans Construction

Size: 2,300 sq. ft.

Location:
Oakland, Calif.

Given the unusual configuration of levels in this house, it was important to make the descent to the lower level an attractive one.

Artful Crafting

The translucent window in the stair alcove is like the jewel at the center of a bracelet. Stained-glass windows like this are ever-changing works of art, with the sunlight creating moving patterns across the walls and floor as the day passes. Given the unusual configuration of levels in this house, it was important to make the descent to the lower level an attractive one. Instead of feeling that you are being pushed down into the basement to sleep, you're given the impression that what's below must be very special to deserve such a marking.

Throughout this house there are many examples of the artful crafting of function. Everything, from the drawers below the window seats to the floating shelves in the living room, has been designed to look effortless and serene. The deceptive thing about this is that to attain such fluidity of form and function requires a lot of up-front planning. There's nothing in this house that hasn't been carefully thought through.

ABOVE If you look at the plan for the master bedroom on p. 211, you'll see that this closet is not only a beautiful piece of cabinetry but also the back wall for the bed's headboard and a divider between the bedroom and the vanity area. We tend to think of walls as the thickness of one stud and cabinetry as something that's pushed up against a wall. Rarely do we think of them as one entity, but there's no reason why they can't be.

OPPOSITE Throughout the house, even on the lower level, there are long connecting views that draw the eye from one end of the house to the other. The corner windows extend the view out beyond the walls. When sight lines are long, the house feels bigger than it really is.

A Not So Big Remodel

DREAMING OF A NEW NOT SO BIG House is all well and good, but for many people the money for such a major undertaking simply isn't available. Adding on or remodeling, however, is often an option, and when accomplished with restraint, it can transform the living environment at an affordable price.

The owners of this house bought their early 1980s rambler because it had wonderful views of Long Island Sound. The house itself was less than wonderful, however, with many of the problems typical of the small, undistinguished ramblers that fill postwar suburbs around the country. It was built from a standard floor plan and designed for a flat lot, but their lot was anything but flat, with a steep slope down toward the Sound. To accommodate the site, the house had been built with a basement and tuck-under garage. But the original builder hadn't stopped to figure out how to get guests and family members up to the main level—where the entry would have been if the house were on a flat lot. It was, for all intents and purposes, a house without a front or back door.

If you can minimize the added square footage and change only the necessities, it's usually less expensive to remodel.

OPPOSITE The new front door is located beneath the main-level deck, adjacent to the garage at left. Most entries bring you into the house at the main level, where the living spaces are, so if you have a lower-level entry, it's important to send guests a clear message that this is indeed the one they should use. The new addition helps give this entry a main-level feel.

ABOVE This 1980s rambler with a tuck-under garage presented some interesting remodeling challenges. The main entry was the three-panel sliding door, just visible on the left of this photo, presenting a wide-open view into the main living space of the house—not a pleasant greeting for either visitor or homeowner. (PHOTO COURTESY CENTERBROOK ARCHITECTS.)

RIGHT A new addition accommodates a master bedroom suite, with office space and an entry below. The deck has been widened slightly to make it work better for sitting and socializing, but the rest of the exterior remains the same—except for a fresh coat of paint and a warmer color scheme. (PHOTO COPYRIGHT JOHN WOODRUFF, WOODRUFF AND BROWN PHOTOGRAPHY.)

The makeshift entry for the family was via a spiral staircase from the garage, winding up into a drafty sunroom off the living room. The space was very tight, making it difficult to bring in groceries, let alone anything larger. Guests had an even stranger entry experience. From the driveway, there was a beautifully landscaped path leading up the hill to what all indications suggested must be the front door. But at the top of the path, visitors found themselves at a wide sliding door, looking directly into the living room. People would turn quickly and descend the path in confusion, assuming they must have missed the proper entry, but this was the only one.

There were a few other problems with the house as well. The kitchen and dining areas were tiny and drab, there was only one bedroom on the main level, and despite its magnificent location,

the house didn't provide places to take advantage of the views. The deck off the dining area commanded the best view of the Sound, but it was too narrow to be of much use. And the exterior color scheme was dark and unwelcoming.

Rethinking the Plan

After living with these problems for a decade, the homeowners decided it was time to remodel. They asked their architect, Jim Childress of Centerbrook Architects, to help them solve their entry problems and to reapportion the space to increase the size of the kitchen, dining area, and bedroom. They also wanted to add a guest bedroom and bathroom somewhere on the main level.

When you are doing major surgery to the structure of an existing house, it can get very expensive. To keep costs down, Jim adopted the time-tested design strategy that says "If it ain't broke, don't fix it." Spend money only where there are problems and leave the rest of the

Architect:
Centerbrook
Architects & Planners

Builder:
Deich Construction
Co., Inc.

Size: 1,950 sq. ft.

Location:
Mystic, Conn.

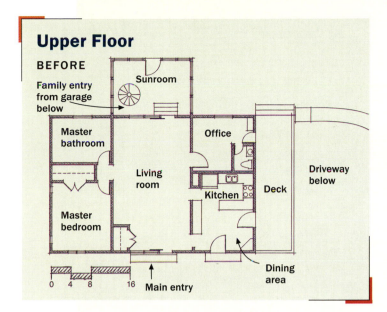

Upper Floor
BEFORE

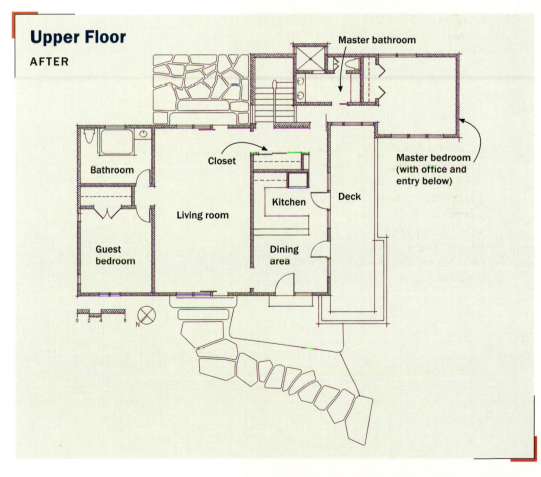

Upper Floor
AFTER

BELOW The brightly painted walls of the stairway and the natural-wood treads give a contemporary flair to the entry sequence. When there's limited daylight, as here, the lighting becomes very important. It's the combination of light and artwork that draws you on to explore the next level.

By adding the new area as a separate structure, the existing roof could remain untouched, which was a major money saver.

house alone. In this case, although the living room and bedroom wing could have been improved, they worked well enough and were left as is.

Jim concentrated instead on the heart of the design problem: improving the entry process for both family and guests. Often it's both easier and cheaper to add on what's needed, especially when there's a need to connect levels, as was the case here. And if one entry could provide both formal and informal access, there'd be less work to be done and fewer associated costs. So Jim proposed building a two-story addition off the northeast corner of the house that would incorporate a new bedroom suite on the upper level, an office space and entryway below, and a stairway to tie everything together.

By adding the new area as a separate structure, connected to the old house by a flat-roofed section, the existing roof could remain untouched, which was a major money saver. And by turning the existing master bedroom suite into the guest suite and placing the new master suite in the addition, Jim gave the couple's private realm a greater sense of remove from the main living areas, as well as better access to the views of the Sound.

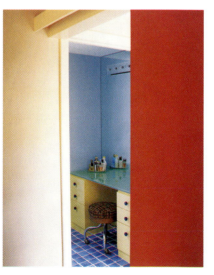

RIGHT The brightly colored sliding door to the right has been made to look like a section of wall rather than a door. It remains open most of the time, but when privacy for the master bedroom suite is desired, the door can be closed.

Moving the office to the lower level of the addition allowed the kitchen and dining areas to be expanded to a more comfortable size. And by keeping the kitchen in the same general area, there was less need for rewiring and plumbing, both major expenses in kitchen remodeling. The remainder of the old office space became an entry closet and landing for the new stairway from the lower-level entry.

An Elegant Solution

The final design has elegantly solved all the old entry confusion with a minimum of means. The new entrance on the lower level, which serves both visitors and family, is next to the office space, with its three big windows creating the look of a main floor. This is enough to give guests the visual cues they need to know that this is indeed the front door. Once inside, even though there are few windows on this level, color and lighting have been used effectively to enliven the space and to draw people up and into the main level—not an easy thing to do gracefully in a constricted space.

ABOVE At the top of the stairs, you can look along the hallway to the new master bedroom suite. The long view helps increase the sense of scale.

Jim's solution may look obvious now, but when you are first contemplating a remodeling, the problems can seem overwhelming and the various needs contradictory. This is why you often see huge additions that don't fit the original house. Rather than taking the time to analyze, develop, and refine a design that does the most with the least, the more typical approach is to solve the problems with square footage. The solution may be expedient, but it's rarely elegant—and often fails to solve the problem.

Making a Little Go a Long Way

An attitude of simplicity and restraint runs throughout this remodeling. The deck, for example, was in perfectly good condition, so rather than tear it off and start over, a new bench was cantilevered out from the existing structure, widening the west corner to create a more comfortable sitting area at a much lower cost than building an entirely new deck.

The kitchen uses sleek but inexpensive custom cabinets with flush doors and very few extras in the cabinet interiors—a strategy that can save a lot of money. Most people don't realize that a custom cabinet is not necessarily more expensive than a stock one. If the door style is simple, requiring only a minimum

ABOVE The original deck was too narrow for anything but a linear arrangement of chairs—not a comfortable way to socialize. By cantilevering a bench from the existing deck, the dimensions have been increased to allow for a sitting circle without rebuilding the deck. (PHOTO COPYRIGHT JOHN WOODRUFF, WOODRUFF AND BROWN PHOTOGRAPHY.)

OPPOSITE/TOP Although the kitchen/dining area is still small even after the remodeling, it seems larger thanks to the long view down the light-filled hallway to the bedroom. Adding French doors along the southwest wall gives the impression that the room extends all the way to the deck railing.

of crafting, and the cabinet interiors don't have a lot of pullouts or other special features, costs can be kept down. And since such cabinets are designed to work with the space available, they can lend the whole kitchen a quality that goes far beyond their cost.

Other features that give this room its personality are the use of color, trim alignment, and unique drawer pulls—all low-cost items. A new refrigerator was not in the initial budget, so an enclosure was made to fit the future refrigerator, which didn't get installed until a year later. If you can allow some small things to be completed as money becomes available, you build in a flexibility that makes it possible to transform your house, over time, into the home of your dreams.

LEFT A trim line extends from the bottom of the upper cabinets over to the raised countertop at the peninsula, defining the upper edge of the backsplash and unifying the design of the room without the expense of another wall of cabinetry.

Move or Remodel?

Whether to move or remodel is a question that most homeowners face at some time in their lives. Like the owners of this house, many people love their location but find their house constricting and inconvenient. Building a new house is an option, but new construction typically costs more than remodeling, even though the actual cost per square foot for remodeled space can be higher than brand new. When you are remodeling, though, there are usually many things that don't need to be redone. If you can minimize the added square footage and change only the necessities, you'll find that it's usually less expensive to remodel.

But if you don't really like where you live and are simply contemplating a remodel because you think it will be easier than moving, think again. Anyone who's remodeled will tell you that living through the construction process is one of the hardest things they've ever done. By all means remodel if you feel connected to a place, but if not, look around for a location that you feel better about.

If you're not sure what to do, consult a local architect and an appraiser or realtor to help you assess your needs and come up with some possible solutions, their probable cost, and the potential increase in property value. Weigh the costs, consider what you will get in return, and you'll be able to determine what makes sense for you.

A Cottage Community

*F*INDING GOOD EXAMPLES OF SMALL houses with the kind of detailing and tailoring that building Not So Big entails was harder than I'd imagined. Finding an entire community of Not So Big houses was an unexpected bonus. Third Street Cottages on Whidbey Island in Washington State is a community of eight tiny houses, located on just two-thirds of an acre. The houses themselves have a main-floor square footage of 600 sq. ft. to 650 sq. ft., with a loft above. They are clustered around a central commons, which includes a lawn and "pea patch" garden. Parking is located in small pockets of three to five cars along the west edge of the property. To enter the neighborhood, you park, come into the commons through an implied gateway, and arrive at each house via its front gate and porch.

The two cottages illustrated here—Hilltop, and Pears and Cherries—give a sense of the overall community and a glimpse of the charm of each individual home. Filled with simple but beautifully designed details reminiscent of the bungalows of the Arts

By spending less on the overall square footage, there's more money available to make a place that's comfortable, well crafted, and personal.

223

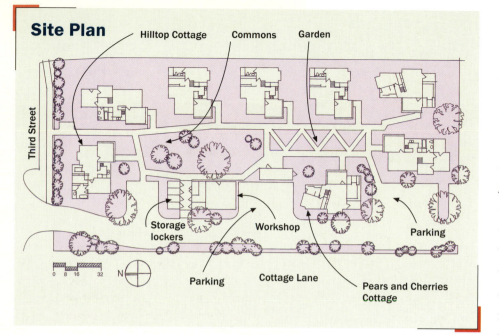

Site Plan

Hilltop Cottage • Commons • Garden

Third Street

Storage lockers • Workshop • Parking

Parking • Cottage Lane • Pears and Cherries Cottage

0 8 16 32

N

and Crafts movement, these homes exemplify what building Not So Big is all about. By spending less on the overall square footage, there's more money available to make a place that's comfortable, well crafted, and personal. Architect Ross Chapin and developer Jim Soules built with this philosophy in mind. As Ross says, "We placed a high value on craftsmanship and design because we wanted to build in character. Yet we didn't want to get too fussy or precious with the details." So they used simple, off-the-shelf items that allowed them to keep costs down while keeping quality and craft up.

Architect:
Ross Chapin Architects
Developer/builder:
The Cottage Company
Size: 710–930 sq. ft.
Location:
Whidbey Island, Wash.

Filled with simple but beautifully designed details, these homes exemplify what building Not So Big is all about.

Nooks and Crannies

The diminutive size of these cottages means that every square foot must be put to use. Rather than making one large, undifferentiated room for the main living area, Ross created alcoves, window bays, and other pockets of space to make a small area seem much larger and to accommodate more activities. For example, Pears and Cherries has a 2-ft. by 10-ft. alcove that increases the usable living-room space by far more than its square footage would suggest. It creates a cozy corner with a lowered ceiling, set off from the vaulted main space.

Other alcoves are smaller still. In Hilltop, there are two tiny bays, each only 16 in. deep. The shallow window bay in the living room brings in more light than if it were flush with the adjacent wall, because the surrounding surfaces reflect the light and bounce it into the room. The window's height from the floor also increases the sense of privacy. The bay in the bedroom

LEFT In the Pears and Cherries Cottage, access to the loft above is via a steep stairway. The bedroom and bathroom are nestled under the loft. The living-room alcove to the left has a lowered ceiling, to distinguish it from the main living area, and the top of the adjacent built-in bookshelves creates a shelf for displaying treasures, which continues around the room.

BELOW Using exposed joists with pine decking instead of drywall gives the ceiling between the bedroom and the loft a lot more character. The window seat shown here is actually more like a skylight seat: The windows are located above ceiling height, bringing in an abundance of light while maintaining privacy from neighboring cottages.

encloses a high window that brings light into the space from above, giving it a warm glow. There's something inspiring about light from above, especially when the source of the light is not visible, as here. It's no accident that this technique was used in churches and cathedrals of the past. But it doesn't take a huge space to create the same uplifting spirit.

A Sense of Entry

This subtle sense of the way spatial experience affects us is evident throughout the cottages. The framed openings for the kitchens in both cottages act as wide doorways, indicating that you are entering a new activity area without obstructing views from one place to another. When space is limited, using this

technique to identify a transition can make a space feel much larger.

An obvious example of this principle is Hilltop's kitchen, seen at right. In the plan, you can see that the room is simply an extension of the living room. Its ceiling height and finish are the same as that of the adjacent space. What distinguishes it as a separate room is the surrounding trimwork and lowered header as you enter. Picture the room without these elements and you can see that the result would look more like a makeshift trailer than a house. It's the detailing, the wing wall adjacent to the refrigerator, and the change in ceiling height that make it work. It doesn't require a dividing wall, just a psychological gateway.

Loft Living

Each cottage has at least one full-height loft, accessed by a steep or alternating-step stair. The lofts provide some bonus space that can be used in a variety of ways—anything from storage space to meditation retreat to home

ABOVE The walls of the Hilltop Cottage kitchen are paneled with reclaimed Sitka spruce. Although the room is small, everything is beautifully detailed. Notice the cabinetry support bracket below the countertop's bar overhang. It's details like this that give a home a personal quality.

OPPOSITE The kitchen in the Pears and Cherries Cottage is designed to be welcoming. Aligning the framed entryway with the window beyond invites you in, and the eating alcove tucked away to the left intrigues you with a glimpse of what's there, making you want to see more.

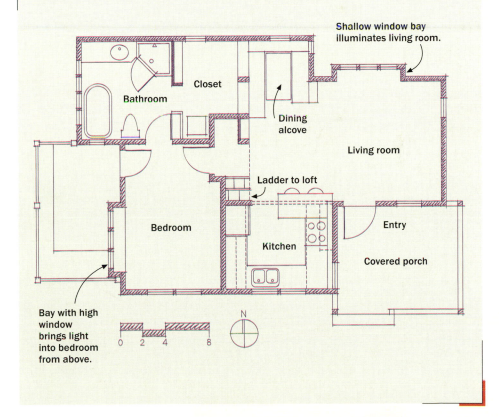

Hilltop: Main Floor

Shallow window bay illuminates living room.

Bathroom

Closet

Dining alcove

Living room

Ladder to loft

Bedroom

Kitchen

Entry

Covered porch

Bay with high window brings light into bedroom from above.

0 2 4 8

N

Although Hilltop Cottage has only 650 sq. ft. on the main level, there's an additional 200 sq. ft. of loft space, room enough for a cozy in-home office. The ship's ladder (a design purportedly invented by Thomas Jefferson) takes up much less space than a standard staircase.

office. The lofts also serve to increase the apparent scale of the main living areas in each cottage by extending the sight lines. When you can see that there's additional living area above and just out of view, it makes the whole main floor seem larger—especially when it's bathed in sunlight.

Building Smaller, Building Smarter

Ross and Jim pared the cottages down to a reasonable minimum in terms of square footage. To give each home its own unique charm, they spent time on design and used materials that had inherent beauty. The houses were also sustainably made, by using fewer resources in their construction than most similar houses built today and materials that are themselves sustainable. The interior walls, which add such warmth to the rooms, are paneled with Sitka spruce that was rejected by a local piano factory and was on its way to a paper mill. The flooring is Medite, a formaldehyde-free particleboard, which has been cut into 24-in. by 32-in. tiles, stained to look like aged leather, and then finished with linseed oil. The exteriors are sided with Hardiplank fiber-cement boards.

These eight houses were designed on spec for singles and couples, a market that is currently largely ignored by mass-market developers. Although more than half of all households in the country consist of only one or two people, almost all new single-family construction is based on a model that's best suited to a much larger family. Despite the fears of lenders, the cottages sold almost immediately, and they have generated enormous interest, both locally and nationally.

Pears and Cherries: Main Floor

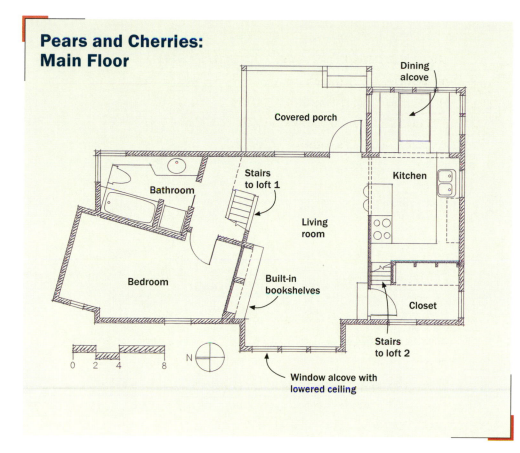

Dining alcove

Covered porch

Bathroom

Stairs to loft 1

Kitchen

Living room

Bedroom

Built-in bookshelves

Closet

Stairs to loft 2

Window alcove with lowered ceiling

0 2 4   8   N

The diminutive size of these cottages means that every square foot must be put to use.

The Cottage-Community Concept

When we imagine the towns and villages of the pre-automobile era, a prominent feature is the strong sense of community that was created by the proximity of homes—and people—to one another. Neighbors went about their daily business on foot, greeting one another or stopping for a brief conversation. People looked out for each other, and a sense of safety prevailed. The Third Street Cottages project taps into this time-honored method of creating community, for those interested in living simply but beautifully.

The project was developed to form a neighborhood with a true sense of home for all of its residents. In order to do this, priority was given to "place making"—creating spots to gather, to work together in the garden, or to greet a neighbor in passing rather than designing around automobiles, as is invariably the case today.

The emblem of our longing for this sort of community is the front porch—such a predominant feature of homes of the past. A porch provides the opportunity to chat with the neighbors or just watch the world go by. Add to this a low split-cedar fence, perennial hedge, and common area, and there's just the right balance between public and private space to allow a community to flourish through the chance interactions of daily life.

RIGHT The cabinetry throughout each house has a personal touch, with simple details added to the door panels and well-chosen hardware, which distinguishes it from run-of-the-mill cabinetry. The painted-wood walls and exposed ceiling joists add far more interest and texture than the standard drywall finishes we're used to.

BELOW When a house is small, you can have light on three sides of a room, an experience you don't get in a larger house, where there is more distance between exterior walls and usually more than one living area in a space. In fact the bigger the house, the darker the middle tends to be.

The days when a single person would never think of buying a home are long past, yet few houses are designed for this large and growing market. And too often, when small houses are built today, they are built cheaply, with little thought to character. But these cottages prove that there are many people out there who want to surround themselves with beauty, comfort, and practicality. And they want their dwellings to reflect their values. A drywalled shoe box just won't do.

ABOVE In the Pears and Cherries Cottage, an alcove surrounded by windows and wide sills provides the perfect ambiance for eating, reading the morning paper, or simply hanging out. It's the cozy size that makes this space work. If it were larger, it would lose the intimacy that makes you want to settle in and relax.

Creating the Dream House

*E*ACH YEAR SINCE 1994, *LIFE* MAGAZINE has asked a prominent architect to design a small, well-crafted home for the American family. In 1999, the firm I was then working with, Mulfinger, Susanka, Mahady & Partners (now known as SALA Architects), was chosen to design the *LIFE* Dream House.

From its experience serving a largely middle-class clientele, SALA realized how little most people understand about how the details in a design can affect costs. To illustrate how costs can vary, the firm suggested that it design not one but two houses: a basic version and a more expensive version of the same plan. *LIFE* Magazine agreed, and two teams of architects at SALA set to work on the designs.

The editors at *LIFE* wanted a house of no more than 2,100 sq. ft., with four bedrooms, all the usual living spaces, and a garage that could either be attached or detached. The firm came

When a house is composed in three dimensions, the interior space can be engaging without it having to cost a lot in the process.

up with a preliminary design in which the main-floor living space was a basic square separated into four quarters—living area, dining area, kitchen, and away room. (The term "away room" was actually coined for this project.) The upstairs was shaped by a large, steeply pitched, triangular roof form—very much like a child's building block in its outline—that overhung the main-level square with substantial eaves. Beyond that, each team was on its own.

The two houses that follow—the Back to Basics version (p. 235) and the Whole Nine Yards version (p. 244)—are the result of this process. They are both based on the same underlying form—a square footprint with a big, sheltering roof above. As you look at each house and refer back and forth, you'll have the opportunity to see just how much difference there can be between houses that, in plan, look very similar.

Basic but Distinctive

Architects Jean Larson and Tim Fuller drew the assignment of designing the Back to Basics version of the Dream House. The challenge was to create a house with integrity and personality while paring it down to its most basic elements. Cost containment was a primary issue for this team, so they decided to keep the form and detailing very simple. Standard materials were used, both inside and out. Interest and spatial variety were introduced with color and lowered soffits—elements that are relatively inexpensive but have significant impact.

Main Floor

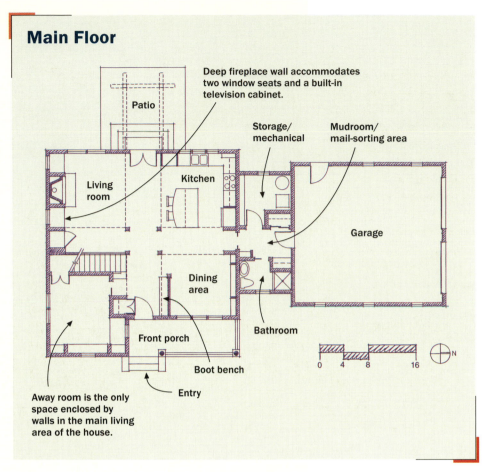

Deep fireplace wall accommodates two window seats and a built-in television cabinet.

Patio

Storage/mechanical

Mudroom/mail-sorting area

Living room

Kitchen

Garage

Dining area

Bathroom

Front porch

Boot bench

Entry

0 4 8 16

N

Away room is the only space enclosed by walls in the main living area of the house.

Upper Floor

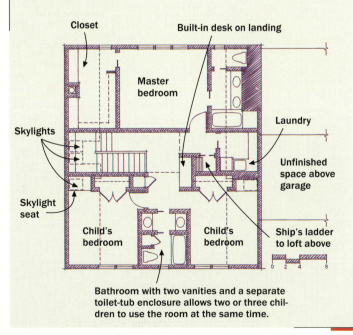

Closet

Built-in desk on landing

Master bedroom

Laundry

Skylights

Unfinished space above garage

Skylight seat

Child's bedroom

Child's bedroom

Ship's ladder to loft above

0 2 4 8

Bathroom with two vanities and a separate toilet-tub enclosure allows two or three children to use the room at the same time.

Architect:
SALA Architects
Builder:
Kyle Hunt
& Partners
Size: 2,100 sq. ft.
Location:
Wayzata, Minn.

Many key principles of building Not So Big combine to make the basic version of the *LIFE* Dream House so successful. With its compact floor plan, which eliminates rarely used spaces like the formal living and dining room, every dollar spent enhances daily life within the home. Nothing is built solely for special occasions. Instead, spaces do double duty: designed primarily for everyday use but easily rearranged for special occasions. The house feels bigger than it is thanks to the long views throughout the house, a key Not So Big technique. You can stand in the corner of the dining area, for example, and see along the diagonal to the far corner of the living room. Or you can stand by the windows in the kitchen and see to the front entry at the other side of the house. If the same space were divided with walls and views were limited, the house would feel considerably smaller.

Designing in the Third Dimension

A primary cost-saving strategy in this house was to keep the "construction logic" fairly simple. A basic rule of thumb in building is that the more corners there are in a house, the more it costs. When you compare floor plans, you'll see that, unlike the Whole Nine Yards version, there are no bump-outs in this house. The basic square of the main house is modified only by the indent for the front entry porch. The upstairs plan is similarly unembellished. But

Thinking Green

One of the goals in this house was to build it as sustainably as possible. Unfortunately, the architects quickly discovered that it is not easy to identify products that are entirely environmentally friendly. Though the market for such products is increasing rapidly and many manufacturers are responding, there's still a lot of work to be done to clarify what is and isn't sustainably made. Since the *LIFE* Magazine project required that all the products used in the house be available nationwide, the design team was able to use only a few sustainable products that are readily available.

The flooring on the main level of the house is bamboo, a material that

is harder than most woods and grows faster than almost any other plant on the planet. It's beautiful too. In the living area (shown here), its changing orientation subtly reflects the soffits above. The cork flooring in the bathrooms and mudroom is an organic material in plentiful supply. And the Hardiplank fiber-cement board siding that sheathes the exterior is more sustainably produced than most other sidings. It's as long lasting and stable as wood but has lower maintenance costs, since it requires less frequent applications of stain or paint. And when used *without* the embossed fake-wood pattern it sometimes comes with, it looks and feels real.

this doesn't mean that the house is boring. When a house is composed in three dimensions, the interior space can be engaging without it having to cost a lot in the process.

If this house had no variation in ceiling height, it would seem bland and little different from a standard tract home. It is the differences in the third dimension, which include variations in ceiling height, special detailing, and built-ins, that make this house distinct from a standard new home. Unfortunately, a typical set of blueprints includes few if any drawings that describe this third dimension. As a result, what gets built is "builder standard"—that is, whatever your builder considers to be the convention of the day.

These days, that doesn't include much variation in ceiling height, other than the obligatory cathedral ceiling in a rarely used formal living room, or perhaps a two-story front foyer. Standard room heights are getting bigger, with 9-ft.- and 10-ft.-high ceilings

With its compact floor plan, which eliminates rarely used spaces like the formal living and dining room, every dollar spent enhances daily life within the home.

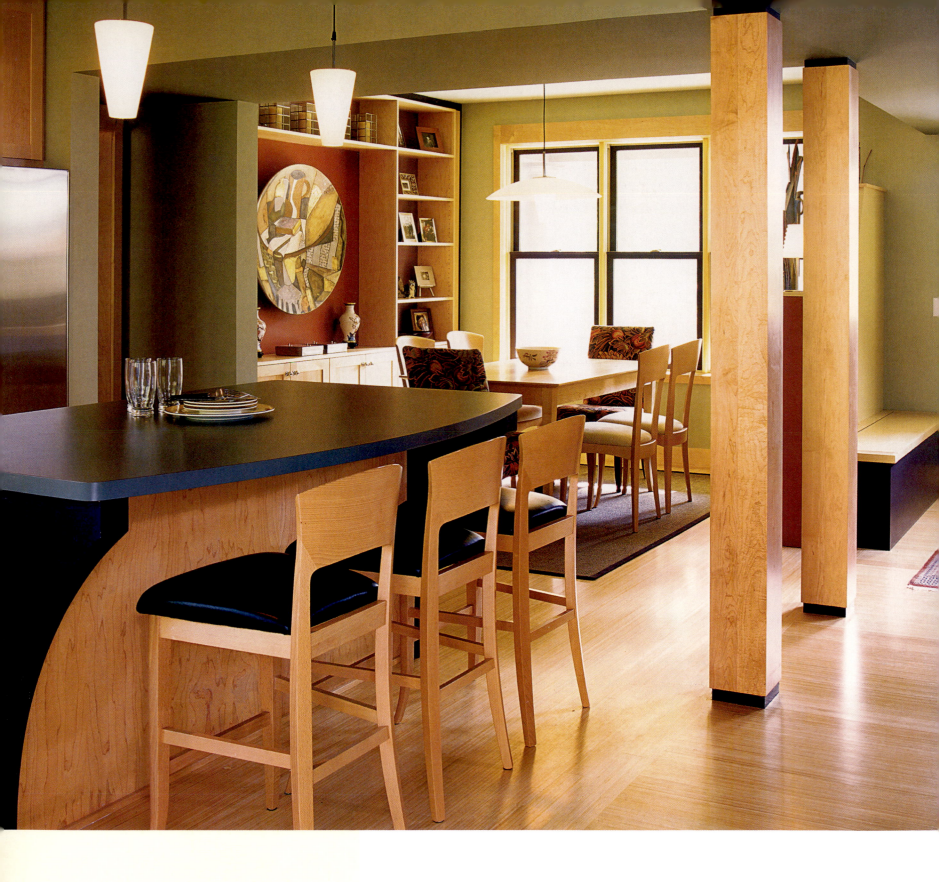

now commonplace. This adds to construction costs but doesn't actually make the space any more interesting than if the ceilings were uniformly 8 ft. high. It's variety that gives a home its character and makes the space comfortable to live in.

Defining Space without Walls

Two long, dropped soffits run the length and breadth of this house—from front door to back door, and from mudroom door to fireplace wall. The soffits divide the plan into four sections and help to give each area a sense of identity without the use of walls. The four columns that mark the intersection of the soffits further define each area and also provide some structural support. Columns can be a wonderful tool for defining space, while allowing you to remove walls and open up sight lines. Unfortunately, many people perceive columns as impediments that block view and movement. But compared to the alternative—a wall—they do just the opposite.

One of the great benefits of building without interior walls is that it allows you the flexibility to move furniture around within the floor plan. Most of the time the furniture in this house remains within the higher-ceilinged areas between the soffits. But when there's a party or a family gathering, the living room couch can be pushed back into the circulation space that connects the front and back doors, and the dining table can be extended into the pathway from mudroom to kitchen. In this way, more people can be accommodated temporarily without building an additional

ABOVE Color and form are used creatively throughout the house to add character but keep costs down. The back wall behind the buffet has been painted with a highly saturated color to draw attention to it and make it appear to be part of a built-in composition. The swooping wall between the dining area and entry is just drywall, but its dramatic shape makes it far more interesting than the typical half wall.

OPPOSITE The floor plan is divided into four quarters—not with walls but with lowered soffits. The columns mark the intersection of the soffits and provide structural support. The kitchen is thus completely open to the dining area, and the space can be used both formally and informally. Countertops are made of plastic laminate—an inexpensive finish—but the shape and design of the island give it the appearance of a more expensive material.

ABOVE The stairway is an excellent place for a row of shelves. If you add 10 in. to the landing—the depth of a bookshelf—you have a ready-made library. This also adds color and texture to a surface that usually goes unadorned.

room for special occasions. In fact, it works better than a house that has these more formal rooms because everyone has access to the kitchen, where the guests generally end up anyway.

The family that moved into this home after it was published in *LIFE* Magazine had previously lived in a much larger house. They bought this one because it had a comfortable, livable practicality that their previous house had lacked. Initially, they were a little worried that the house might feel tight, but to their surprise, it actually seemed more spacious, both when they were together as a family and when they had guests. Although the living space was significantly smaller in square footage, it was all usable, all the time. That's one of the most surprising aspects of building Not So Big. With decreased square footage, it's assumed that the house must inevitably feel a bit tight. But it doesn't. The measurable dimensions are smaller, but the psychological dimensions are bigger.

Getting Away from It All

The only room enclosed by walls in the main-level square is the away room, designed to offer a place of quiet respite and also to serve as a study and occasional guest bedroom. In a house as open as this one, it's important to have an enclosed space, especially when there are young children in the family. In a typical floor plan, the quiet room is often the living room, which is usually too big and too formal for everyday use. The away room offers a cozy and comfortable retreat that can serve a variety of needs. This is a good example of a space in which bigger is clearly not better.

By creating two alcoves in the room—a built-in desk and a window seat—the room can serve on a daily basis as a study, a quiet place to read, or a spot to sit and watch the world go by. The two soffits and adjacent shelving help define the alcoves as distinct from the rest of the room, even though the spaces are very small. When guests come to stay, the couch can be folded out into a bed without obstructing the desk space, and the window seat serves as an excellent suitcase platform.

Nooks and Crannies

There are other tiny alcoves here and there around the house. Often the most heavily used spaces in a house are the throwaway corners that no one ever really plans. In a Not So Big House, these corners are acknowledged and designed for, so they become highly usable and enjoyable places to be. Usually located between flanking walls, and with either a lowered ceiling or raised floor, these spaces offer a sense of shelter around the activities they house.

ABOVE The away room serves multiple functions, working as a study or quiet retreat and as an extra bedroom when guests are staying over. The two alcoves help make the room work for both occasions. Eliminate the shelves and the dropped ceilings, and the room would be bigger but less able to support all these activities. Either the desk or the window seat would have to go.

This compact children's work area has been carved out of leftover space on the landing. Set beneath the ship's ladder to the attic above and flanked by a narrow end wall, the desk has been given its own alcove. Without the sense of enclosure provided by the wall and the lowered ceiling, the desk would seem out of place.

One such space is found at the top of the stairs, where a desk is built into the space below the ship's ladder to the attic. It's located close to the kids' bedrooms, where both children can use it, and is a perfect location for playing computer games or doing homework. By making the built-in desk a part of the circulation space, it doesn't take up nearly as much area as if it were placed in its own separate room. The sloped wall of the stair above, far from being a problem, makes this space all the more delightful.

There are more wonderful nooks in each child's room. Rather than running the closets all the way to the exterior wall, there's a skylight seat (instead of a window seat) tucked into the space between the kneewall and the closet. Locating the skylight directly adjacent to the back wall brings a flood of light into this cozy spot. It's just the kind of space that children love to make into their own little cocoon—and it takes up only 6 sq. ft.

Paint Is Cheap

One of the most notable characteristics of this house is its color scheme. If all the walls and ceilings were white, it would seem much less interesting. Here the color palette is bolder than most, with the highly saturated colors— deep terra-cotta and primrose yellow—used only for special accents. Look at the fireplace wall, for example (see the photo on p. 232). The fireplace surround is drywall, just like all the other wall surfaces in the house. It is in-

dented 1½ in. and painted with an accent color, making it the focal point of the wall. The expense of tile or stone was avoided, but the color gives it plenty of impact.

The same color is used behind the buffet in the dining area (see the photo on p. 239), making the entire wall appear to be a special built-in element, when in fact the amount of cabinetry (and associated cost) is limited. The use of the same color as a design accent in different rooms also ties the whole house together. In the bathroom upstairs, instead of using tile on the walls, a narrow trim band encircles the room at the height of the countertop, and the areas above and below are painted two different colors.

"Paint adds definition and energy to spaces," says Jean. "It does in a less expensive way what costly details can do." For many people who are trying to save some money in the construction of their homes, painting is one of the very last tasks and can even be done by the homeowners themselves, if necessary. Using color in this way adds a lot of character inexpensively and can be accomplished over time, as energy allows. And if you don't like it, it's easy to change.

The use of the same color as a design accent in different rooms ties the whole house together.

LEFT A niche for a skylight seat has been made between the closet wall and the side wall of the house in this child's bedroom. Aligning the skylight with the back wall of the seat and painting it a light color makes the whole surface a reflector, bouncing light into the room and making a delightful place for a child to play.

Up Close

There are alternatives to tile for bathroom floors and walls. Here, a narrow band of trim divides the room into upper and lower sections, and a simple change of color adds lots of personality without the expense of tile. The floor is made of cork, a natural and sustainable material.

The Whole Nine Yards

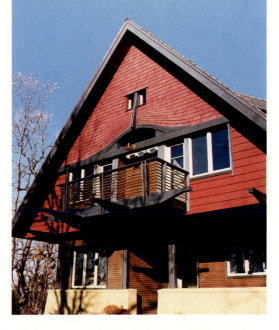

WHEN YOU LOOK AT THE MAIN-LEVEL floor plan for the upgrade version of the 1999 *LIFE* Dream House (known by the architects at SALA as the Whole Nine Yards house), you can see the generic similarity to the basic house (see pp. 246 and 236, respectively). There are the same four quadrants, the indented front porch, and the front door that lines up with the French doors opening to the backyard. The garage and mudroom are in the same position. You may notice that the upgrade plan is just slightly larger, that this house does have some bump-outs, and that the dining area and kitchen are reversed. Surely these aren't such significant differences. Yet the interior of the house looks quite different, and the cost of this house is substantially higher than the basic house—almost double, in fact. To find out why, let's evaluate the house piece by piece and analyze the differences between the two versions.

ABOVE The triangular gable set on the smaller square of the main level carries on the child's building-block motif, but unlike its less-decorated sibling, this version of the Dream House is intricately detailed. The gable end is symmetrical and almost seems to have a face, composed of windows and trim. A balcony with oversized brackets extends beyond the front porch, accentuating the entry.

There's a quality of constant discovery in this house, an effect created by layering, which is one of the basic techniques that makes Not So Big work.

OPPOSITE With a masonry fireplace set at an angle, adjacent built-ins for the television and stereo, and a view through the screen porch to the St. Croix valley below, this living room has everything—a fabulous view, an old-world intimacy, and easy access to the TV set (which is concealed from view when the cabinet doors are closed).

Main Floor

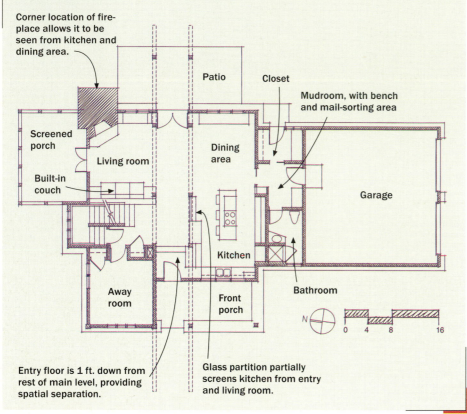

Corner location of fireplace allows it to be seen from kitchen and dining area.

Patio

Closet

Mudroom, with bench and mail-sorting area

Screened porch

Living room

Built-in couch

Dining area

Garage

Away room

Front porch

Kitchen

Bathroom

N   0 4 8   16

Entry floor is 1 ft. down from rest of main level, providing spatial separation.

Glass partition partially screens kitchen from entry and living room.

Architect:
SALA Architects
Builder:
Derrick Construction Co.
Size: 2,500 sq. ft.
Location:
Afton, Minn.

A House from Memory

The form of this house has a lot more detailing—what architects call "articulation"—than the basic house. This means that there's more depth, an effect created by the application of various materials to the surface. Look at the front face of the house, for example. There's the indented porch on the main level, just as on the other house. But there's also a smaller indented deck on the second level and an eyebrow created with shingles and trim above the second-floor windows, giving the house a wonderfully expressive face. The stucco base of the house stands proud of the walls by several inches and is flared out to make a solid-looking platform. As architect Michaela Mahady puts it, "It makes it feel as if the house is growing out of the ground." And then there are the dormers, which, when combined with the broad overhangs, call to mind a chalet in the Austrian Alps. All these elements add a unique quality and craft to the house, but of course each one also adds to the cost.

The alpine motif is no accident. The house sits high on a bluff overlooking the St. Croix valley, and Michaela used imagery from her own cultural memory (she has family roots in Austria) to make a house that, for her, is evocative of

home and comfort. Together with architects Wayne Branum and Katherine Hillbrand, she created a house that has an intimate feel and a sense of surprise around every corner. Like a good book, it makes you want to keep reading—to explore every nook and cranny and discover all its secrets.

The interior is welcoming and rich in both color and texture. As in the Back to Basics house, there's a lot of color used throughout, though here it is in a darker, more subdued palette. But there the similarity ends. Whereas expensive finishes were avoided in the Back to Basics house in favor of color, here materials such as wood and stone have been employed to give the

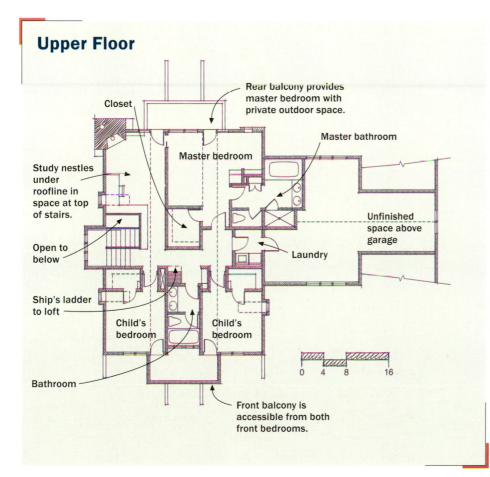

Upper Floor

Closet

Rear balcony provides master bedroom with private outdoor space.

Master bedroom

Master bathroom

Study nestles under roofline in space at top of stairs.

Open to below

Unfinished space above garage

Ship's ladder to loft

Laundry

Child's bedroom

Child's bedroom

Bathroom

0   4   8   16

Front balcony is accessible from both front bedrooms.

ABOVE The master bedroom has a cabinlike feel, with lots of wood paneling and a spectacular view of the valley. The bed sits in an alcove created by a lowered ceiling that's 7 ft. 6 in. from the floor. The alcove makes a cozy pocket of space in a room with an otherwise tall ceiling.

OPPOSITE The strong, simple form of the roof with its accompanying dormers evokes the image of an alpine chalet. Though it is reminiscent of vernacular architecture, it is anything but a reproduction. This is a design that learns from the past but transforms it into an innovative image for today.

home its warmth. When budget constraints are less of an issue, such natural materials can add a timeless quality and character to a house. But they're not critical to livability or personality; their effect is simply different.

Enduring Quality

The dropped ceiling that cuts through the center of the house is made of wood, where drywall was used in the basic version. And, although the usual wood casing is omitted around the windows, there's a lot of wood used in other places, with a plethora of built-ins and paneled walls and ceilings. Much of this wood was salvaged from the bottom of Lake Superior, where huge tree trunks have languished for centuries. Wood retrieved in this manner is of a caliber and hardness seldom found today and is an excellent sustainable material, but it comes with a hefty price tag. When built into a house like this one—a house designed to last for centuries—it will provide pleasure for many generations to come.

Rooms in the Roof

The ceilings throughout this house are higher than in the basic version, with an extra foot of height on the main level and the sloped form of the roof expressed in each room on the second level. This is a detail that costs more than standard 8-ft.-high ceilings but adds wonderful spatial complexity. Unlike the cavernous cathedral ceilings typical of suburban houses today, however, these sloped ceilings spring from a height that is more proportioned to human scale. In the study at the top of the stairs, for example, the ceiling comes down to 5 ft. behind the desk, rising

ABOVE A comfortable study opens off the stairway landing on the second floor, a change from the basic house, where the upper level was significantly smaller. The darker colors of the painted walls and woodwork add to the intimacy of the space, and the ceiling seems to wrap down around the desk area, giving a sense of shelter to the activities below.

OPPOSITE The kitchen is designed for informal eating and is partially screened from the living room by a glass partition. The kitchen island is designed to be a functional work surface, an informal eating area, and a work of art. The raised section can also serve as a buffet during parties. The countertop material, a product called Fireslate, feels wonderful to the touch and looks like stone, though it's actually a combination of portland cement, silica sand, and fillers.

ABOVE The entryway is open to the main level but sits two steps down. The built-in bench provides a place for removing shoes, a feature that's particularly welcome in snowy Minnesota. As family and friends come and go, the photos displayed here tell something of the lives of the inhabitants—a simple personal touch.

RIGHT The screen between the stairway and the kitchen, made of obscuring glass, protects the entryway from direct views into the kitchen work area. The columns supporting the two beams that run the length of the house have an unusual and elegant design, giving the whole composition an Asian flavor and simplicity.

to 12 ft. at the peak, and then descending back to 10 ft. on the other side of the room.

If you look at the section through the house on p. 253, you'll see that the slope could in fact have risen all the way to the wall opposite the desk, but in so doing the room would have lost all its coziness. Like a sculptor, an architect manipulates the space available to make every room into a place of comfort, beauty, and functionality. Just because the space is available doesn't mean that it will improve the room to include it. As with a well-tailored suit, often the fabric that is cut away is as important as the fabric that appears in the final article.

Layer upon Layer

There's a quality of constant discovery in this house, an effect created by layering, which is one of the basic techniques that makes Not So Big work. When talking about this effect, Michaela mentions an inspiration from her childhood. At Eastertime, she was sometimes given a large, scenic Easter egg. The egg was made with layer upon layer of spun sugar, suggesting a scene below and another below that. By breaking away the layers, she would discover more and more about the marvelous creativity of its making. A house can do the same thing.

As you walk through the front door, to your right is a wall that's not really a wall at all. Composed of built-ins and obscuring glass, it invites you to explore, just like the Easter egg. You want to know what's behind it, but you are also

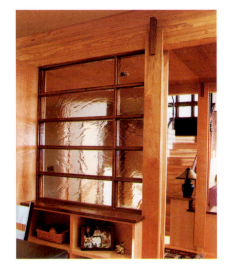

By crafting every surface and sculpting every space, the whole house becomes a work of art, as well as an extraordinarily comfortable place to live.

drawn to the wall itself. You might stop and look at the pictures on the photo-display shelves. You might look through the peekaboo opening into the kitchen to catch a glimpse of the activities within. Or you might press your nose against the glass and enjoy the distorted view through to the kitchen island. How much more interesting than just a plain old wall made of studs and drywall.

Entering from the garage, you also have a clear sense of the layering that underlies the home's design. As you enter through the mudroom—a space complete with mail-sorting area, backpack storage, and walk-through closet—you see past the kitchen and the glass wall, past the column marking the edge of the stair, to the living room beyond. Although the distance is only 34 ft., it feels much greater, because of the layers you're looking through. They engage you, draw you into the house, and make you want to explore. The more layers you see, the more intriguing it becomes.

On the upper level, the layers are not quite as intricately detailed, but they still allow a sense of flow and an awareness of the whole as well as the parts. The transom windows above each door are a good example of this. The frameless glass tricks the eye into believing there's nothing there. The vault and roof ridge seem to extend endlessly, making the house seem significantly bigger than it really is, while the wall still does its job of providing acoustical and visual privacy where it's needed.

What Makes a House Expensive?

The two versions of the *LIFE* Dream House—the Back to Basics (BTB) house and the Whole Nine Yards (WNY) house—beautifully illustrate the relationship between complexity and cost. By comparing the two, you can see just how much difference quality of materials and complexity of design can make. Both houses are similar in size—the WNY house is just 400 sq. ft. larger—and have similar floor plans, yet the WNY house is almost twice as expensive to build as the BTB house.

The following features contribute to the difference in cost between the two. As you look through this list, refer back to the plans and photos for each house to see the differences.

On the exterior, the WNY house has an intricately detailed pattern of cedar shingles at the gable end walls, with narrow lap siding below, as compared with Hardiplank fiber-cement board siding for the BTB house. The WNY house has a massive stucco chimney for a full masonry fireplace instead of a side-venting gas zero-clearance fireplace insert requiring no chimney at all. There are shed dormers on the WNY house, which greatly increase the complexity of the roof framing, versus easy-to-install skylights set between trusses in the BTB house.

On the interior, the WNY house has more woodwork, more built-ins, and a multitude of custom-crafted details. By contrast, the BTB house uses paint color for character instead of woodwork, and a limited number of built-ins in places where they'll have the greatest effect. The WNY house has Fireslate countertops and high-end appliances, whereas the BTB house has laminate countertops and mid-range appliances.

Spatially the houses are quite different, too. There are several bump-outs on the WNY house that make the foundation more expensive to build. It has higher ceilings throughout, with an opening between the main and upper floors adjacent to the staircase; exterior balconies from the bedrooms; and vaulted ceilings on the second level that add to the structural complexity. The BTB house keeps the ceilings at a standard 8-ft. height and omits the balconies and the opening between levels. It is also designed without a basement, allowing the space below the upper run of stairs to become part of the living room, which in turn reduces the length of the house by several feet.

Often we are unaware of the increased complexity caused by a bump-out in a foundation wall or an increase in ceiling height. If your goal is to keep costs down, make sure that the materials you use are consistent with your budget and that every effort is made to keep the structure simple to build.

Although this house is expensive, with a cost per square foot substantially higher than a typical home today, much of what makes it so livable comes from the quality of the design rather than the cost of the materials. Of primary importance is the fact that this home offers many more places for real living to occur than many much larger homes. By crafting every surface and sculpting every space, the whole house becomes a work of art, as well as an extraordinarily comfortable place to live. This is an intimate house, a house that embraces both its inhabitants and guests with its presence.

Back to Basics House

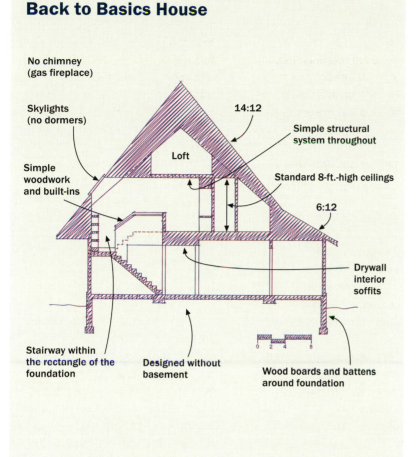

No chimney (gas fireplace)

Skylights (no dormers)

14:12

Loft

Simple structural system throughout

Simple woodwork and built-ins

Standard 8-ft.-high ceilings

6:12

Drywall interior soffits

Stairway within the rectangle of the foundation

Designed without basement

Wood boards and battens around foundation

0 2 4 8

Whole Nine Yards House

Massive stucco chimney

Varied ceiling heights on upper level

14:12

Shed dormers

8:12

More complex structural system required by varying ceiling heights.

Interior soffits have beams and wood veneer.

Highly detailed woodwork and built-ins

9-ft.-high ceilings

Stairway and several other areas are bumped out from the rectangle of the foundation, adding complexity.

Designed with full basement

Battered walls around base of house with stucco finish

0 2 4 8

LIFE Magazine asked SALA to put forth its vision for the house of tomorrow. In both versions, the answer is clear: a smaller, more tailored home that has a floor plan designed for today's informal lifestyle, with as much craft and personalization as the budget permits, built with sustainable techniques and materials that will allow the house to last for centuries. It's a far cry from the typical house of today. And it won't become the norm until we stop building big and start building Not So Big, tailoring our houses to become the homes our spirits crave.

OPPOSITE The transom windows above each bedroom door allow light and view to flow between spaces, while still providing an acoustical barrier. With no surrounding frame, the eye is fooled into believing there's no membrane at all. The roof seems to continue unobstructed, and the space seems larger as a result.

Afterword:
The Plans for the Houses

THE BEST WAY TO GET A HOUSE
that really fits you and your site is to hire an architect.
Of course, it costs more to have a custom design made
just for you—usually from 5% to 15% of construction
costs, depending on the kind of service—and it takes
significantly more time and effort than the alternatives,
such as selecting a plan from a home-plans magazine or
from your builder's standard options. But the result can
more than repay the effort: a tailor-made home you'll
feel is an extension of your own life.

A significant segment of the home-buying public
wants the level of quality and craft that architectural
drawings afford but doesn't want to invest either the
time or the money required for a custom design. These
people want the quality that comes with the Ralph
Lauren or Liz Claiborne label, without having to hire
Ralph or Liz themselves. Unfortunately, unlike the
fashion industry, there are few such options in the
residential-housing marketplace. You can either buy
generic, or you can hire the artist directly. This leaves a
huge middle ground that is almost completely unserved
in today's marketplace.

These people need a new way to select a house
design, based on images of the interior as well as the
exterior and with ample description of the three-
dimensional character of the spaces within. The plans
for the houses in this book are being made available
with this goal in mind. What distinguishes them from
those you would normally buy from a plan book is the
level of detail included and the overall quality of the

designs. The hard work that gives a house the kind of effortless beauty you see in these homes begins long before construction starts. Where a set of plan-book blueprints might be typically 4 to 6 sheets long, it is not unusual for an architecturally designed home to have 20 or more sheets, illustrating all the special details that make everything work together as a unified whole.

But it's not really the number of sheets of drawings that matters; it's the quality of thought and ingenuity that goes into the design process. We tend to think of house design as something easy and obvious, because we have lived in houses all our lives. But for something to have both functionality and beauty, it must be molded, sculpted, tailored, and proportioned with an artist's eye. The resulting drawings are simply the means to record all of that planning and communicate it to the builder.

When you are considering purchasing plans that are this highly detailed, it's important to remember that making a change to the floor plan—even a small one—can have ramifications that are not readily apparent but can dramatically change the look and feel of both the interior and exterior. Frequently, people will make such a change, thinking they are making an improvement, only to discover that in so doing they have spoiled much of what they loved about the house. So if you purchase a set of detailed plans and want to make an alteration, I would strongly advise that you contact an architect to help you. You may need to make more modifications than you realize.

People often ask which they should select first—the site or the house plan. The answer is *always* the site. You will want to make sure that your house design is suitable for your site; oriented to take advantage of views, vegetation, and sunlight; and tailored to the contours of the land. An architect can be very helpful in assessing the appropriateness of a design and in fitting the house to your site.

Although architects have traditionally been disdainful of the home-plans market, this is changing as we observe with dismay what is happening in our suburbs. It is estimated that architects are involved in only 2% to 3% of all houses built today. Making good design available to a larger market is the best way to turn the tide away from ever larger and increasingly uninteresting megahouses and toward homes with more style, character, integrity, and soul. If the response to my first book is anything to go by, there are a lot of people eager for a better approach to home design. What we have to do is fill the vacuum and bring some designs of quality into the marketplace. Our dreams of home are seldom generic. Why should the houses we build be so? It's time for a change.

Architects and Designers

A Timeless Classic
Peter Twombly, AIA
Estes/Twombly Architects, Inc.
79 Thames St.
Newport, RI 02840
mail@estestwombly.com
interior designers: Peter Twombly
and Lisa Ballou

A House for Today and Tomorrow
Murray Silverstein,
with Bill Mastin
Jacobson Silverstein Winslow
Architects
3106 Shattuck Ave.
Berkeley, CA 94705
jswarch@aol.com

The Essence of Home
Jeremiah Eck, FAIA
Jeremiah Eck Architects, Inc.
560 Harrison Ave., Suite 403
Boston MA 02118
www.jearch.com

Doing More with Less
Matthew Schoenherr, AIA
Z:Architecture
61 Jesup Rd.
Westport, CT 06880
zarchitecture@prodigy.net
interior designer: Beth Schoenherr,
Sheridan Interiors

A Farmhouse for Our Time
Jean Larson, AIA, with
Steve Mooney
SALA Architects
43 Main St. SE, Suite 410
Minneapolis, MN 55414
www.salaarc.com

A Jewel in the Suburbs
Jim Garramone
Garramone Design
9 Williamsburg Ct.
Evanston, IL 60203-1828
garrdesign@aol.com

Three Easy Pieces
Frederick Phillips, FAIA
Frederick Phillips &
Associates
1456 N. Dayton St., Suite 200
Chicago, IL 60622
fpaarch@interaccess.com

A Sense of Flow
Bernie Baker
Bernie Baker Architect, P.S.
5571 Welfare Ave., NE
Bainbridge Island, WA 98110
bba@bainbridge.net

A House in Harmony
Paul Lukez, AIA, with
Jim Bruneau, Steve Beaucher,
and Mark Fuller
Paul Lukez Architecture
7 Davis Sq., Studio #10
Somerville, MA 02144
www.lukez.com
interior designer and colorist:
Gale Lindsay
landscape architect:
Claire Batchelor
lighting: Michael Eberle, Chimera
artist in metal: Roger Chudzik

Affordable Comfort
Ross Chapin
Ross Chapin Architects
P.O. Box 230
Langley, WA 98260
www.rosschapin.com

Comfort, Pueblo-Style
Daniel William Hoffmann, AIA
DWH Architects, Inc.
P.O. Box 1157
Taos, NM 87571
www.taosfolk.com/dwhoffmann

Thinking outside the Box
Barbara Winslow
Jacobson Silverstein Winslow
Architects
3106 Shattuck Ave.
Berkeley, CA 94705
jswarch@aol.com

Playfully Sustainable
Ted Montgomery
Indiana Architecture & Design
477 Ten Stones Cir.
Charlotte, VT 05445
www.indiana-architecture.com

One Phase at a Time
Robert Knight, AIA
Knight Associates
P.O. Box 803
Blue Hill, ME 04614
www.knightarchitect.com

Updating a Not So Big House
Barry Svigals, AIA
Svigals Associates
5 Science Park
New Haven, CT 06511
www.svigals.com
interior designer: Art Osborne

Tight Quarters
Josh Heitler
Lacina Group, Architects
141 E. 3rd St.
New York, NY 10009
lacina@msn.com
designer, bathroom wall:
Mark Womble

Southern Comfort

Eric Moser
Moser Design Group, Inc.
P.O. Box 7931
Hilton Head Island, SC 29938
mdgi@rhsnet.com
developer: Bob Turner,
Habersham Development Co.
residential designer: Eric Moser,
Moser Design Group, Inc., and
OCM Architecture
interior designer: Cris Taylor,
Plantation Interiors

An Accessible House for One

Geoffrey Prentiss, AIA
Prentiss Architects, Inc.
1218 6th Ave. W.
Seattle, WA 98119
prentissarch@earthlink.com

P.O. Box 1537
Friday Harbor, WA 98250

A Place of Cool Remove

Sharon Tyler Hoover, AIA
Sharon Tyler Hoover,
Architect
12 E. Davidson
Fayetteville, AR 72701
shoover@nwark.com

Elegant Simplicity

James Estes, AIA
Estes/Twombly Architects, Inc.
79 Thames St.
Newport, RI 02840
mail@estestwombly.com
cabinetmaker: Joe Yoffa

Upstairs, Downstairs

Murray Silverstein, with Chet
Zebroski and Andrea Traber
Jacobson Silverstein Winslow
Architects
3106 Shattuck Ave.
Berkeley, CA 94705
jswarch@aol.com

A Not So Big Remodel

James Childress, AIA,
with Mark Herter and
Thomas Salmaso
Centerbrook Architects &
Planners
P.O. Box 955
Centerbrook, CT 06409
www.centerbrook.com

A Cottage Community

Ross Chapin
Ross Chapin Architects
P.O. Box 230
Langley, WA 98260
www.rosschapin.com

Creating the Dream House (Back to Basics)

Jean Larson, AIA, Timothy
Fuller, AIA, Sarah Susanka,
AIA, and M. Christine Johnson
SALA Architects
43 Main St. SE, Suite 410
Minneapolis, MN 55414
www.salaarc.com

The Whole Nine Yards

Michaela Mahady, AIA,
Katherine Hillbrand, AIA,
Wayne Branum, AIA, and
M. Christine Johnson
SALA Architects
904 S. 4th St.
Stillwater, MN 55082
www.salaarc.com

The house featured on pp. iii, 7,
9 (top), 10, 12, 13 (bottom), 17, 18,
and 19 was designed by:

Sarah Susanka, AIA
www.notsobighouse.com

Ordering Information

The Taunton Press is pleased to offer complete blueprints for sale for most of the houses featured in this book. For additional information about plan pricing and services to alter the plans to your specific site, needs, and local requirements, please contact the plans fulfillment center at HomeStyles.com. You can order by phone or online (please do not contact the individual architects directly):

Phone orders (toll free)   (877) 370-1364
Online orders   www.creatingnsbh.com

The following house plans are available for sale:

A Timeless Classic (TP01:TWO-01)

The Essence of Home (TP01:ECK-01)

Three Easy Pieces (TP01:PHI-01)

A House in Harmony (TP01:LUK-01)

Affordable Comfort (TP01:CHA-01)

Comfort, Pueblo-Style (TP01:HOF-01)

Playfully Sustainable (TP01:MON-01)

One Phase at a Time (TP01:KNI-01)

Southern Comfort (TP01:MOS-01)

An Accessible House for One (TP01:PRE-01)

A Place of Cool Remove (TP01:TYL-01)

Elegant Simplicity (TP01:EST-01)

A Cottage Community :

　　　Pears and Cherries Cottage (TP01:CHA-02)

　　　Hilltop Cottage (TP01:CHA-03)

Creating the Dream House: Back to Basics (TP01:LDH-1999-B)

The Whole Nine Yards (TP01:LDH-1999-W)

In addition, plans for the author's house (featured on pp. iii, 7, 9 (top), 10, 12, 13 (bottom), 17, 18, and 19) are also available (TP01:SS-2444).

Photo Credits

Bernie Baker: p. 87 (bottom)

Centerbrook Architects: p. 216 (top)

© Grey Crawford: cover; pp. i–iv, v–vi, 1–2, 4, 6–7, 8 (left), 9–25, 26 (right), 27–28, 31–34, 36–39, 41–42, 43 (bottom), 45–47, 48 (right), 49–50, 52, 55, 56 (top), 57–70, 72–79, 81–86, 87 (top), 88, 90–97, 98 (left), 99–103, 105, 107–109, 111 (left), 112–115, 117–123, 125–127, 129 (top), 130–134, 135 (left, top right), 136–143, 145–152, 155–164, 166–171, 173–179, 181–186, 188–190, 192 (bottom), 193–197, 199–205, 207, 208 (bottom), 209, 211–215, 218–219, 221–224, 225–233, 238–252, 254

Jeremiah Eck: front flap; pp. 8 (right), 40, 43 (top), 48 (left)

Hester and Hardaway Photographers: pp. 187, 192 (top)

Jacobson Silverstein Winslow: pp. 124, 128, 129 (bottom), 206, 208 (top), 210

Warren Jagger: pp. 26 (left), 30

Paul Lukez: p. 98 (right)

Charles Miller (courtesy Fine Homebuilding **magazine, © The Taunton Press, Inc.):** pp. 104, 106, 111 (right)

Ted Montgomery: p. 135 (bottom right)

David Ottenstein: p. 153

Robert Perron: p. 144

Frederick Phillips: p. 80

Scott Phillips (© The Taunton Press, Inc.): back flap

Prentiss Architects: p. 180

Matthew Schoenherr: p. 51

Sarah Susanka: p. 237

© Candace Tetmeyer: p. 56 (bottom)

John Woodruff, Woodruff and Brown Photography: pp. 216 (bottom), 220